FRANKLIAN PSYCHOLOGY IN CHRISTIAN SPIRITUAL FORMATION

by
Randy L. Scraper, PhD

FRANKLIAN PSYCHOLOGY IN CHRISTIAN SPIRITUAL FORMATION

by

Randy L. Scraper, PhD

Copyright ©2009 by Randy L. Scraper

ALL RIGHTS RESERVED. No part of this book may be reproduced, stored in a retrieval system, or transmitted by any form or by any means, electronic, mechanical, photocopying, recording, or otherwise, except as may be expressly permitted by the applicable copyright statutes or in writing by the publisher

ISBN: 978-1-55605-394-8

Library of Congress Control Number: 2009922518

WYNDHAM HALL PRESS
Lima, Ohio 45806
www.wyndhamhallpress.com

Printed in The United States of America

This work is dedicated to my wife, Wanda, who has shown unrelenting support for all of my endeavors, academic and otherwise. I have great appreciation for her willingness to discuss and cooperatively evaluate every tenet of the propositions that form the corpus of thought for this project.

Randy L. Scraper

Acknowledgements

There are so many people who deserve to be listed in this section of acknowledgements because of the influence they have had upon my life. I am only sorry that I can list so few.

Miss Ethel Archer, my Jr. High history teacher gave me an undying appreciation for becoming a renaissance person. Her teaching and that of Mrs. Nadene Percy, gave me a desire to pursue an education in the liberal arts that guided me to Baker University. My parents, Robert and Vida Scraper, supported my desire to go to school with encouragement and financial help. Their values have shaped my own in such wonderful ways.

Viktor Frankl was mesmerizing from the first time I heard him. I said then, and still say now, that here is (was) a man that made sense. His influence upon my life has been nothing short of fantastic! I can still remember saying to myself when leaving the first of his lectures at Baker University, "I want to keep track of this man and his work, and I will." Indeed I have, and it has been one of the great joys of my life.

Elisabeth Lukas has been a significant influence with her writing and with her teaching. Her encouragement has meant a great deal to me. Robert Barnes has been "the hound of heaven" for my continued involvement in Logotherapy. Even though I have needed little if any persuasion, his tenacity has been warmly appreciated. Paul Welter has shaped and guided my studies in Logotherapy as well as given me much practical advice through his wise counsel and genuine care.

Several persons have contributed their expertise and love to the shaping of my Christian life. James Hewett has been a dear friend as well as mentor in my Biblical studies. He also gave me a genuine appreciation for the English style of education. Hobart Hilyard was a pastor and role model during some of my most formative years. He showed me how much fun it can truly be to be a Christian.

I owe more than words are adequate to express to two persons, Benedict Groeschel, whose work in exposing the framework of "the three ways" has changed my life in so many ways, and Ann Graber, who has been a wonderful Ordinarius as well as a superb teacher and friend. Her writing and her conversations have meant a great deal to me.

I owe more than could ever be expressed to my lovely wife, Wanda, whose faithful support has enabled all of my work in Logotherapy as well as every other area of my life. Her life has given me an overwhelming sense of meaning and purpose which nothing but our life with God could possibly match.

I am more grateful than words can express for all of these persons and for the many more whose names are not mentioned here. Their absence from these pages in no way detracts from their influence upon my life or from my appreciation for them.

Randy L. Scraper

Introduction

The purpose of this book is to examine the formation, benefit, and use of a meaning matrix for Christian spiritual formation through the application of Franklian psychology (Logotherapy) and Franklian philosophy (Logo philosophy) to the time-honored method of Christian spiritual formation known as the three ways. The book begins with a short history of Viktor Frankl's life and an explanation of Franklian psychology and philosophy.

The problem addressed in this book is the lack of knowledge concerning the significant transitions in the Christian spiritual life and the resultant lack of practice of a meaningful method for Christian spiritual formation among the rank and file of Christians. The book addresses the way in which the application of Franklian psychology and Franklian philosophy to the three ways provides a meaningful understanding of the significant transitions of the Christian spiritual life. The book includes an overview of the widely accepted understanding of Christian spiritual formation known as the "three ways." Significant foundations for this view are provided in the works of Evelyn Underhill, Benedict Groeschel, and Adolphe Tanquerey.

This research study was conducted with Christians who are members of the United Methodist Church. Many of the participants have also been members of other denominations with some having been members of as many as five Christian denominations over their lifetimes. The information in this book shows how people are most likely to overrate their initial knowledge of Christian spiritual maturity and how an understanding of the Meaning Matrix helps to move Christians toward a deeper understanding and practice of Christian spiritual maturity.

The book provides an interesting and in depth view of how a meaningful understanding of Christian spiritual maturity can flow from the application of Dr. Viktor Frankl's Logotherapy and Logo philosophy to the time honored practice of Christian spiritual formation known as the three ways. Anyone interested in developing a more meaningful understanding of Christian spiritual maturity will find this book very helpful.

Randy L. Scraper

CONTENTS

Acknowledgements..........2
Introduction...................4

CHAPTER I
Overview....................9

CHAPTER II
Primer of Viktor Frankl's Life.............16

CHAPTER III
Franklian Dimensional Ontology 65

CHAPTER IV
Franklian Methods of Meaning Discovery ..940

CHAPTER V
The Three Ways of Christian Spiritual Formation …..104

CHAPTER VI
Current Appl. of Psychology to the Three Ways…142

CHAPTER VII
Franklian Psychology, the Three Ways, and the Meaning Matrix ……………. 152

CHAPTER VIII
Are Christians Really Helped By This Information? 168

CHAPTER IX
Application and Uses of the Meaning Matrix ….172

CHAPTER X
Conclusion ………………………….178

Appendix A 181
Appendix 183
Appendix C........................187
Appendix D.........................197
References............................ 201
Bibliography........................208

LIST OF FIGURES

Figure 1 50
Figure 2 51
Figure 3 69
Figure 4 70
Figure 5 72
Figure 6 76
Figure 7 79
Figure 8 91
Figure 9 153
Figure 10 154
Figure 11 156
Figure 12 160
Figure 13… 164

CHAPTER I
OVERVIEW

Christians from the first century forward have intentionally sought spiritual formation in the image of Christ. The search has been referred to as a "journey" by some and a "quest" by others. Those who highlight the process and practice of spiritual formation gravitate toward defining it as a journey. Those who see the possibility of being formed in the image of Christ in this lifetime gravitate toward defining it as a quest. Both groups would benefit from a better understanding of the times of transition in the Christian spiritual life. This understanding is exactly what is offered through the establishment of a meaning matrix for Christian spiritual growth through the use of Franklian psychology.

For one to best understand the contributions of Franklian psychology in the formation of this meaning matrix, it is necessary to have an acquaintance with the life of Dr. Frankl, the principles of Logotherapy, and, in particular, the addition of the noetic dimension to the ontological view of the human being. A cursory understanding of these important factors allows one to better grasp the deeper meanings of Frankl's human dimensional ontology and be able to rightly relate it to the methods of meaning discovery and the three ways of Christian spiritual formation.

The establishment of a meaning matrix for Christian spiritual formation through the use of Franklian psychology helps people have a clearer understanding of the purpose of Christian spiritual formation and of the significant transitions in the Christian spiritual life. Without the help of a meaning matrix that Franklian psychology can provide, Christians interested in further developing their spiritual life are often at the mercy of the latest spiritual fad. When Franklian psychology is understood in conjunction with the time-honored understanding of Christian spiritual formation known as the three ways, the significant transitions in Christian spiritual formation are more recognizable and better understood.

In the fall of 1969, I entered Baker University in Baldwin City, Kansas, as a freshman to discover that the entire curriculum was developed around Dr. Frankl's book and was called, *Man's Search for Meaning*. For the first three years of the college experience at Baker University, students studied general education courses that were organized around the theme of *Man's Search for Meaning* to discover the many ways in which the arts and sciences could work together when viewed from this perspective.

Baker University was (and is) a United Methodist university, founded in 1858, and preparing to celebrate its 150th anniversary this year. It was while a freshman there that I learned the theories of Logotherapy and met Dr. Frankl while he spent several days lecturing and visiting with the students in various classes as well as informal settings. *Man's Search for Meaning* was required reading and was consumed by the student body. Dr. Frankl's lectures were "standing room only" in Rice Auditorium, the largest facility on campus at that time.

I can still remember leaving the first lecture Dr. Frankl delivered and saying to myself, "This makes more sense than almost anything I have ever heard. I am going to keep track of this guy and see what he has to say." This commitment was enhanced during the class sessions that were held with Dr. Frankl for those of us who were in philosophy and religion courses. Little did I know at that time how this commitment would lead to a life-long fascination with Dr. Frankl and his teachings. In the years following I would join and serve as an officer in the Mid-West Institute of Logotherapy as well as serving on the board of the Viktor Frankl Institute of Logotherapy. I would have the privilege of leading workshops and delivering addresses at the World Congress(es) on

Logotherapy held in Dallas and later in Toronto. For nine years I served as an adjunct professor at Baker University's Kansas City campus of the School of Professional and Graduate Studies where I would teach Logotherapy in the Department of Philosophy and Religion. During the years preceding my time in Kansas City, I was living in Topeka, Kansas, where I was able to access the Menninger Library and acquire copies of all of the published copies of Viktor Frankl's articles. It was during that time that I learned enough German to read and translate his articles that were published only in German.

Through all of this time my assessment of Dr. Frankl has remained the same. Indeed, "This makes more sense than almost anything I have ever heard. I am going to keep track of this guy and see what he has to say." This fascination most logically led me to an interest in determining how Logotherapy and Logo philosophy relate to Christianity and enhance the meaning of spiritual formation in the life of a Christian. This interest has been followed with a strict adherence to Dr. Frankl's own desires voiced in an address to a class on World Religions at Baker University so many years ago when he said that just as Logotherapy was a complement to psychotherapy and not a component of psychotherapy, Logotherapy was a complement to religion rather than a component of a religion. Dr. Frankl indicated his own interest in seeing people of various religions develop understandings of the ways in which Logotherapy and its foundational tenets could further enhance the meaning of religions around the world.

Dr. Frankl's lifelong appreciation for the mystery of "coincidence" is directly connected to the formation of the tenets of Logotherapy. It is this acknowledgement of the presence of the human spirit and the mystery that its presence introduces into human dimensional ontology that opens Logotherapy and Logo-philosophy to an extremely fruitful interaction with Christianity and, in particular, Christian spiritual formation.

I have conducted research throughout my life that systematically explores the hypothesis that Christians would benefit from the formation of a meaning matrix as a result of the application of Franklian psychology to the method of Christian spiritual formation known as the three ways. This book is a result of the findings from that research. In Chapter II you will find an examination of the foundational principles of Franklian psychology including a short history of Dr. Frankl's life, the principles of Logotherapy, and an examination of the addition of the noetic dimension. This examination includes the freedom of the will, the will to meaning, and meaning in life as the principles of Logotherapy. It also covers the Greek roots for the philosophy that underlies Dr. Frankl's thinking in this area. Some knowledge of all of these items is necessary for a fundamental understanding of the meaning matrix. In Chapter III you will find a critique and extension of Franklian dimensional ontology that is necessary to the understanding of the meaning matrix. The tri-partite and transcendent nature of Dr. Frankl's view of human dimensional ontology is examined and explained. The integrated nature of human dimensional ontology is also addressed with a focus on volition, rationalization, conceptualization and revelation. These concepts define the activity of the human being in the critical areas of transition between the human dimensions.

In Chapter IV you will find descriptions of the methods of meaning discovery taught by Dr. Frankl. These include discovery through experiential values, creative values, and attitudinal values. Much of the information found in Chapters two through four comes from primary sources written by Viktor Frankl, Elisabeth Lukas, Ann Graber, Joseph Fabry, William Gould, James Crumbaugh, James Yoder and others, as well as previous study with the Viktor Frankl Institute of Logotherapy.

Chapter V is an overview of Christian spiritual formation through understanding the three ways. The historic view of the three ways is examined through the writings of Benedict

Groeschel and Evelyn Underhill. Other primary sources include writings by Thomas Merton, Adrian Van Kaam, and Adolphe Tanquerey. An explanation is given of the Purgative, Illuminative and Unitive ways with a discussion of the types of prayer that are consistent with each of these three ways. The types of prayer include petition, meditation, meditative-contemplation, contemplative-meditation, simple contemplation, the prayer of full union, the prayer of passive union, and infused union. This information will be interesting and detailed for those who are seeing it for the first time. It will be a significant review for those who have previous knowledge of the three ways.

In Chapter VI we will examine the current application of psychology to the three ways. It is here that the work of Benedict Groeschel adds so much to our understanding. He has done significant work in the application of a deeper understanding of psychology as applied to the three ways. His book <u>Spiritual Passages</u>, published by Crossroads Press, is a classic in this field.

Chapter VII describes the development of the meaning matrix. The Franklian dimensional ontology axis and the spiritual formation axis are described and the primary methods of meaning discovery for each of the human dimensions during the movement through the three ways are examined. It is important to note and to remember that the meaning matrix defines the transitions of the Christian spiritual life by focusing on the **primary** methods of meaning discovery. Each of the methods of meaning discovery may be at work in each of the human dimensions, but the key to understanding the transitions of the Christian spiritual life is found by focusing on the primary methods of meaning discovery and **how they shift within the human dimensions** during the process of Christian growth and maturity.

I have developed and led a number of workshops focused on the formation of the meaning matrix. These workshops included both a Pre and Post-Workshop Questionnaire. The Pre and Post-Workshop Questionnaires were created by soliciting information from valued colleagues in the fields that are germane to this subject. In order to create the most meaningful Pre and Post-Workshop Questionnaires possible, a Spiritual Formation Workshop Evaluation Questionnaire was distributed to twenty people; five logotherapists, five theological educators, five psychologists, and five pastors. The return rate was 100%. The answers given were averaged and those questions which received an overall rating of important, very important, or essential, were included in the Pre and Post-Workshop Questionnaires.

At the workshops, the participants were invited to complete both the Pre and the Post-Workshop Questionnaires. Participation was about 90%. Those who completed both questionnaires were included in this study. The information gathered was compiled and compared. Chapter VIII contains the analysis of this research which concludes that a knowledge of the meaning matrix provides a more meaningful understanding of the significant transitions in the Christian spiritual life and will have a positive affect upon Christian spiritual growth.

Chapter IX discusses the application and uses of the meaning matrix. I strongly believe that significant benefits will be provided to Christians who are moving through spiritual formation when those working with them in the helping professions such as pastors, spiritual guides, spiritual friends, educators, and those in the healing ministries, have a working understanding of the meaning matrix. Christians will grow forward in their spiritual maturity in a more meaningful way when they can better understand and even anticipate the significant transitions that they will experience. I believe that well informed and experienced pastors, spiritual guides, spiritual friends, educators and persons involved in the healing ministries will serve a truly meaningful purpose by helping

Christians better understand, move into and move through these significant spiritual transitions. An understanding of the meaning matrix will prove to be a great benefit to those who help Christians grow forward spiritually.

    In Chapter X, I suggest that additional study in the area of the application and use of the meaning matrix would be beneficial. I also suggest that the study be expanded. This expansion would provide a broader base for the research and development of the use of the meaning matrix. I believe that the principles that have been discovered in the formation of the meaning matrix will prove to be beneficial to all who work with human spiritual formation. Both application and further study will be helpful in the further development of the meaning matrix as a truly helpful aid in understanding, fostering, and nurturing Christian spiritual growth.

CHAPTER II
FOUNDATIONAL PRINCIPLES OF FRANKLIAN PSYCHOLOGY

The principles that create the foundation of Franklian psychology were formed in the early years of Viktor Frankl's life, honed to deeper meaning during the tumultuous years of survival, and proven during his long and honored life of service. These principles were forged in the fires of interaction with the Freudian and Adlerian schools of psychology as well as his horrendous sufferings while incarcerated in four concentration camps. They were the product of "standing on the shoulders of giants" to see further down the road ahead. They were also the product of a radical testing that only the circumstances of his life could have verified.

Primer of Viktor Frankl's Life
The Element of Coincidence

The mold was cast early in the life of Viktor Frankl. He was born in 1905 in Vienna, Austria. The events of his young life would both mold his thinking and prove his theories. These same events would cause him to confess, at the least, an appreciation for irrefutable coincidence and, at the most, recognition of the mystery involved in the possibility of a "higher, or deeper, ultimate meaning" (Frankl, 1997, p. 57). In his own words, Frankl would write that:

> I think the only appropriate attitude to such coincidences is to not even try to explain them. Anyway, I am too ignorant to explain them, and too smart to deny them (Frankl, 1997, p. 59).

These "coincidences" began early in Frankl's life. He writes about the time when he was two years old and wandered away from his parents at a train station. He walked out onto the tracks in front of a stationary train that was being loaded with passengers. It was not until the whistle blew that his father realized he was no longer near and rushed out onto the tracks to snatch his young son from in front of the train.

Frankl decided at the age of three that he wanted to become a physician, much to the delight of his father. In the early years of his life he vacillated between several types of medicine. His early interest in psychology helped him make the decision to become a psychiatrist. In March of 1938, only a few months after Dr. Frankl had opened his private practice, Adolph Hitler's troops marched into Austria and changed the social structure of the country. Frankl was a Jew and as such was only allowed to treat Jews.

Dr. Potzl, a party member who was "far from being anti-Semitic" was helping Dr. Frankl as he manipulated the diagnoses of mentally ill patients to save them from the forced euthanasia that had been ordered by the Nazis for all the mentally ill. Dr. Frankl recounts this practice in his own words;

> I circumvented that law by certifying schizophrenia as aphasia (an organic brain disease) and melancholia as fever delirium (not a psychosis in the strict sense of the word). This protected the administrators of the home though it put a noose around my own neck. Once the patient was placed inside the protective bars and netting on the bed, schizophrenia could be treated with cardiazol shocks or a phase of melancholia could be overcome without suicide risk (Frankl, 1997, p. 81).

One day after picking up a Jewish man and woman for transfer to a home for the elderly using their cooperative scheme, Dr. Frankl was riding with a social worker behind the two taxis that had picked up the man and woman, one patient in each taxi. Dr. Frankl noticed that one of the taxis turned right to go to the nursing home while the other, the one with the woman in it, turned left to go to the Steinhof mental hospital. When he asked why, the social worker explained that the lady had recently converted from Judaism and was no longer allowed to go to the nursing home. Dr. Frankl wrote that a shiver ran down his spine when he realized what circumstances could turn into a "death sentence" for the lady who would now be taken from the mental hospital to the gas chambers (Frankl, 1997, pp. 81-82).

Not many years later, a young Dr. Frankl would be thrilled to learn the news that his long awaited immigration visa to the United States had finally been granted. The struggle of whether or not to leave his parents behind became almost unbearable. He knew that they would soon be deported to the concentration camps and die in the gas chambers. The visa applied only to him. Frankl's own words best describe the next "coincidence".

> Undecided, I left home, took a walk, and had this thought: "Isn't this the kind of situation that requires some hint from heaven?" When I returned home, my eyes fell on a little piece of marble lying on the table.
> "What's this?" I asked my father.
> "This? Oh, I picked it out of the rubble of the synagogue they have burned down. It has on it part of the Ten Commandments. I can even tell you from which commandment it comes. There is only one commandment that uses the letter that is chiseled here."
> "And that is . . . ?" I asked eagerly.
> Then father gave me this answer: "Honor thy father and thy mother, that thy days may be long upon the land which the Lord thy God giveth thee."
> Thus I stayed "upon the land" with my parents, and let the visa lapse.
> It may be that I had made my decision deep within, long before, and that the oracle was in reality only an echo from the voice of my conscience. This is to say, it may have been a kind of projective test. Someone

else may have seen in the same piece of marble nothing but $CaCO_3$ (calcium carbonate). But would that not have been his projective test also, perhaps in his case of existential emptiness (Frankl, 1997, p. 83)

This decision set in motion a series of events that defined the life and message of Dr. Frankl from this point forward. He would lose his father, his mother, his brother and his wife to the gas chambers of the concentration camps. He and his sister would be the only members of his family to survive this holocaust. Yet even in the tortures of this hellacious existence, coincidence would continue to play its significant role.

Dr. Joseph Mengele, one of the Holocaust's most notorious mass murderers, was selecting prisoners: to the right for labor in the camps, and to the left for the gas chambers. In my case, Mengele pointed my shoulder toward the left. Since I recognized no one in the left line, behind Mengele's back I switched over to the right line where I saw a few of my young colleagues. Only God knows where I got that idea or found the courage.
Entering Auschwitz, when I was required to discard my own, perfectly good coat, I took an old, torn one. It had apparently belonged to a person who had been gassed. In a pocket I found a leaf, torn from a prayer book. On this scrap of paper was the principal prayer of Judaism, the *Shema Israel* ("Hear, oh Israel, the Lord our God is One"). How else could I interpret this "coincidence" than as a challenge to me *to live* what I had written, to practice what I had preached (Frankl, 1997, pp. 93-94)

In addition to losing his coat, Dr. Frankl lost his manuscript of *The Doctor and the Soul*, which was sewn into the lining of his overcoat in hopes that it would be protected there and survive the punishment of the concentration camps. A large part of his will to survive the concentration camps was a direct result of his desire to be able to reproduce this manuscript and publish his book. It was, however, his short account of his experiences in the four Nazi concentration camps, which he dictated in nine days that catapulted him onto the international stage. This little book, *Man's Search for Meaning*, has now been translated into 24 languages. Five times, various American colleges have chosen it as "the book of the year".

The Early Years of Psychological Development

While growing up in Vienna, Viktor Frankl had the distinct privilege of experiencing the joys of a middle-class Austrian upbringing and then the terrible realities of poverty and oppression. No one describes the dichotomy of this experience better than Ann V. Graber in her book, *Viktor Frankl's Logotherapy: Method of Choice in Ecumenical Pastoral Psychology* and William Blair Gould in his book, *Frankl: Life With Meaning*. They both recognize the high quality of Frankl's early education.

Austria was the recipient of the foresight of Josef II, the Hapsburg Emperor who mandated public education for all children in the year 1790. As a result of this mandate and the efforts to carry it forward, Austria boasts the University of Vienna founded in 1368 and a literacy rate of 99% (Graber, 2004, p. 23). Viktor Frankl was the recipient of a high quality education that by its structure forced the decision early in life to choose either a professional, a para-professional, or a vocational field of training. Frankl was pleased to take advantage of the "professional" track in education and chose to become a physician specializing in psychiatry. His life-long love for learning was evidenced in his earning his M.D. degree in 1930 at the University of Vienna and continuing to complete a Ph.D. degree in Philosophy in 1949. His list of honorary doctoral degrees is exceptionally long and distinguished.

The 1918 armistice combined with the dissection of the nation of Austria created great deprivation on the part of the Austrian people. This deprivation was felt across the entire population. As a youth, Frankl had to join his family in begging for food at the farmer's market in Vienna.

He tells of stealing corn from the fields when he and his family visited relatives in Moravia. Thus, as a boy entering his teens, he identified with the social and economic needs of the poor. It is understandable that in latter years the young Frankl was attracted by the work of Sigmund Freud (1856-1939), who considered himself a world reformer as well as a leader of a new science of the self called psychoanalysis (Gould, 1993, pp.1-2).

In junior high school, Frankl began taking adult night courses in psychology and developed a keen interest in anything dealing with psychology. He began writing letters to Sigmund Freud about anything that Frankl had happened across which he thought might interest Dr. Freud. To his astonishment, Dr. Freud answered each letter and encouraged Frankl's continued studies in the field. In Frankl's own words, it was while:

. . .I sat on a park bench in the Prater Park – my favorite working place at the time – and put down on paper whatever came to my mind regarding the origin of the mimic movements of affirmation and negation."
I enclosed the manuscript in a letter to Freud. I was more than surprised when Freud wrote to me that he had sent my article on to the *International Journal of Psychoanalysis,* hoping I would not object.
And indeed, later on, in 1924, it was published in that journal (Frankl, 1997, pp. 49-50).

Frankl did not agree with all of Freud's theories or practices and it is well known that while Freud's theories of psychotherapy were based on his assumption of a *will to pleasure* on the part of human beings that *drove* human actions,

Frankl saw the fundamental force as one that *led* rather than *drove* human actions and was based on a *will to meaning*. Frankl was fond of saying that even though he disagreed with much of what Freud taught, he believed that Freud was a giant influence in the field of psychotherapy. Frankl also often stated that even a dwarf (*Zwerg*) standing on the shoulders of a giant could see further than the giant could see. He compared himself to that dwarf and Freud to the giant.

Sigmund Freud

Ann V. Graber adds an important dimension to the understanding of the development of psychological thought from Freud through Adler to Frankl by focusing on the social milieu in which each of the "Viennese schools of psychotherapy" were birthed and found their greatest significance. She states . . .

> A Viennese, Stephen Kalmar, gives us an on-site observer's view of the changing political and cultural currents of Vienna during those times. Growing up during the Austro-Hungarian Monarchy, Kalmar knew the Imperial Vienna – the city of Freud. He also witnessed the tumultuous years subsequent to the fall of the Habsburg Empire, the struggle for freedom and the search for identity – the city of Adler. He furthermore experienced Vienna when the search for meaning in the midst of chaos was paramount – the city of Frankl (1982, xv – xxiv). The history of a new school of thought is, in its first phase, largely the history of its founder. A closer look at the historical and cultural milieu of the founders of the three Viennese schools of psychotherapy and their corresponding ideologies will bear this out (Graber, 2004, p. 4).

Sigmund Freud was 49 years Frankl's senior and at the prime of his career when Frankl was communicating with him.

The years of a highly structured, authoritarian, autocratic society in Austria were rapidly passing, but those years had served as the backdrop for the development of psychotherapy and its discovery of the subconscious, its exploration of the drives and instincts experienced in the human condition, and the explanation of the reaction formations that formed the core of psychoanalysis. It had been a time of strict adherence to structure and a pietism that left little or no room for freedom of thought and expression.

> Repression of authentic feelings often presented symptomatically as hysteria, which was socially more acceptable than disagreement with the status quo of the society (Graber, 2004, p. 4).

In the early part of the 20th century, Freud's psychoanalytical circle included some amazing thinkers. Sabina Spielrein, Alfred Adler, and Carl Jung were among those that helped Freud think through the thoughts that became foundational tenets in his book, *Beyond the Pleasure Principle,* published in 1920. In this book Freud states that we are often caught between the motivation toward happiness and the replaying of earlier events in our lives. He concludes that we are moving forward often thinking we are "growing toward a life unified by love (eros), . . .(while) . . . we are actually being driven toward the disintegrating powers of decay or death (thanatos)" (Gould, 1993, p. 3).

Freud's influence early in the life of Viktor Frankl is displayed in the fact that, although still a teenager at the time, Frankl was lecturing to hundreds of youth in youth clubs about the relationship between sexual problems and meaning. Frankl was a deep thinker and a brilliant conversationalist as evidenced by his ability to comprehend and interact with the arguments of both Freud and Jung concerning the battle between the life-death dualism presented by Freud and monistic theory of the libido presented by Jung. It was in 1922 that Frankl "conceived the importance of ultimate meaning for the self; and as Frankl states 60 years later, 'this concept accompanied me throughout my life and stood the test of the concentration camp'"(Gould, 1993, p. 3).

As the situation in Austria deteriorated and the Nazis prepared for *Anschluss* on March 12, 1938, Freud finally admitted that Austria was finished. Only one month earlier he had expressed his admiration for the way that the Austrian government was standing up against the Germans and was complimentary of Chancellor Kurt von Schuschnigg saying he was "decent, courageous and a man of character (Gay, 1988, p. 618).

Within two days of *Anschluss*, the Nazis searched Freud's home and office. They were looking for any evidence of an "international conspiracy". Late in March of 1938, Freud finally relented of his position to stay in Austria. He had desired to stay due to his ill health, suffering from cancer of the mouth and jaw. Following the confiscation of his passport and the arrest of his daughter, Anna, he decided to immigrate to England.

At the age of 82, Freud continued to fight against the Jewish scholars who disagreed with his writing *Moses and Monotheism,* and he started *Outline of Psychoanalysis,* the last message to his colleagues, encouraging them not to let psychoanalysis "stagnate". Finally, Freud indicated his desire to become a British citizen "possibly because of his long affection for England and his reception there as an emigrant but more probably because of his final rejection of Austria. As in so many of his personal relationships, love had turned to hate" (Gould, 1993, pp. 6-7).

Alfred Adler

Alfred Adler was the next great influence in Frankl's life. Adler was, at one time, the "favorite son" and "heir apparent" of Freud's psychoanalytic movement. Austria had changed greatly by the time Alfred Adler was coming of age in the psychoanalytic community. World War I had changed Austria forever. The Hapsburg Empire had collapsed. "An empire of sixty-million people had been reduced to a small nation of six million" (Graber, 2004, p. 5). A new Austrian republic was emerging.

Although most of the remaining Austrians were Catholic and strongly conservative, a new government of Social Democrats was emerging in the heart of Vienna. This new Social Democratic party was much more liberal, anti-traditional, and socialistic. It espoused new freedoms that were never a part of the old Austrian experience. These new freedoms created a society set adrift in the middle of an "existential vacuum".

Alfred Adler was dismissed from the Freudian circle when he took issue with some of the fundamental assumptions made by Freud and demanded of his followers. While Freud espoused a theory that was based on biological and environmental determinants, Adler sought more freedom for the establishment of identity. Adler did some medical research independent of the Freudian circle and discovered what he considered to be good reasons for moving in a different direction than the one that was demanded by Freud. This new direction resulted in the formation of Adler's individual psychology.

Viktor Frankl experienced the deprivations that World War I brought to the Austrian people. He and his family knew what it meant to suffer privations and to survive. When Adler was creating his "second Viennese school of psychotherapy", Frankl was entering the University of Vienna where he would not only become a Social Democrat, like Adler, but he would go on to become the president of the Social Democratic student movement in 1924 (Graber, 2004, p. 7). Frankl became one of the youngest members of Adler's circle and the Association for Individual Psychology.

Frankl agreed with Adler on many points. His greatest agreement was around the belief that "freedom of choice" was central to a person's ability to make decisions. This freedom became a central element of Franklian thought and in the development of Logotherapy. It is rather ironic that Adler was forced from Freud's circle due to his (Adler's) development of this belief and yet when challenged at a critical point later in his life, Adler would in turn expel Frankl from his circle for expanding this very belief.

Frankl's belief in the power of the individual to find meaning in the face of unavoidable suffering grew from the foundation of the exercise of volition on the part of every individual. Frankl saw this as a trait that was uniquely human. He maintained the belief that there should be room in psychological circles for differences of opinions without the need to expel those who held such opinions. Adler did not agree.

The influence of Albert Adler and the eventual deterioration of their relationship are best described in Frankl's own words:

> In 1925 my article "Psychotherapy and World View" was published in his (Adler's) *Journal of Individual Psychology*. In 1926 another one followed. The same year I was asked to give the keynote address at the International Congress for Individual Psychology in Dusseldorf, but I could not do so without deviating from the orthodox line of the congress. I denied that every neurosis, always and everywhere, is a mere means to an end in the sense of the doctrine of its "arrangement character." I insisted upon the alternative to see it not as a mere "means," but also as a symptom, which means not only in an instrumental, but also in an expressive sense. . . . In 1927 my relationship with Adler deteriorated. I had come under the spell of two men who impressed me not only as persons, but who also had a lasting influence on me through their ideas: Rudolf Allers and Oswald

Schwarz. I began to work under Allers at his Laboratory of the Physiology of the Senses. Schwarz, founder of psychosomatic medicine and a medical anthropologist, did me the honor of supplying the foreword for a book I was asked to write for the Hirzel publishing house. It never saw the light of day because, in the meantime, I was expelled from the Society for Individual Psychology (Frankl, 1997, pp. 60-61).

This expulsion was obviously problematic for the young Viktor Frankl. He goes on to describe it in detail.

Then came the evening in 1927 when Allers and Schwarz were openly to announce and to justify their withdrawal from the Society for Individual Psychology, a decision that they had earlier made known privately. The session took place in the large lecture hall of the Histological Institute of the University of Vienna. In the back rows sat a few Freudians, who enjoyed the spectacle of watching Adler experience the same fate that Freud himself met when Adler withdrew from the Society for Psychoanalysis. Here again was a "secession." The presence of psychoanalysts made Adler all the more sensitive.

When Allers and Schwarz had concluded their remarks, there was a heavy tension in the air. How would Adler react? We waited in vain. Embarrassing minutes passed. I was seated near Adler in the first row. Between us sat one of his students, whose reservations about Adler's ideas were as well known to Adler as my own reservations. Finally, Adler turned to us and scoffed, "Well, you heroes?" What he wanted to say was that we should have the courage to show our true colors by speaking up.

So I had no choice but to step up in front of everyone present and to explain how individual psychology still had to free itself from psychologism. And I made the mistake of declaring myself, right in front of the "enemy" psychoanalysts, in favor of Schwarz and even called him "my teacher." It was not much help that I asserted that I saw no reason to leave the Society for Individual Psychology because I believed that we members could overcome our psychologism. In vain I tried to build bridges between Allers, Schwarz, and Adler.

From that evening on, Adler never spoke a word to me again, never acknowledged my greetings when, on many evenings, I approached his table in the Café Siller where he held court. He could not get over the fact that I had not supported him unconditionally.

Repeatedly he had others suggest to me that I should resign from the society, but still I saw no reason for that. A few months later I was expelled formally (Frankl, 1997, pp. 62-63).

Viktor Frankl

Viktor Frankl came of age during a time of tremendous turmoil. He was a medical student in 1929 when he developed his concept that there were three basic groups of values through which meaning could be found. He understood these as:

1.) a deed we do, a work we create; 2) an experience, a human encounter, a love; and 3) when confronted with an unchangeable fate (such as an incurable disease), a change of attitude toward that fate. In such cases we still can wrest meaning from life by giving testimony to the most human of all human capacities: the ability to turn suffering into a human triumph (Frankl, 1997, p. 64).

Frankl was in his late twenties and engaged to be married when he made one of the most far-reaching decisions of his life. He decided to cancel the visa, which would have allowed him to immigrate to the United States and flee the wrath of the Nazi holocaust that was looming. His own sister had already immigrated to Australia. His parents and friends had advised him to immigrate as soon as possible. He believed that, as a psychiatrist, he could protect his family, but soon discovered that such belief was futile.

He struggled with the decision to leave his parents and his homeland. It was an inner turmoil unlike any he had weathered previously.

> Covering the yellow star that he was compelled as a Jew to wear, he entered Saint Stephen's Church in the center of Vienna, where an organ concert was taking place. He sat in a pew and prayed silently, "O God, give me a sign." Should he stay with his family with the hope that they could be saved, or should he go to the United States, where he believed he could continue his pioneer work in psychology? When he came home he found his father in tears. When Frankl asked his father what had happened, his father replied, "Viktor, the Nazis have destroyed the synagogue" and showed him a fragment of marble he had salvaged. The fragment of the Torah his father held in his hands had one letter engraved on it, the beginning of the commandment "Honor thy father and thy mother." Frankl called the American embassy and canceled his visa. He had received his sign (Gould, 1993, p. 7).

Viktor Frankl continued to develop his ideas about "the border area that lies between psychotherapy and philosophy, with special attention to the problems of meanings and values in psychology" (Frankl, 1997, p. 59). As a result, the "primary motivation" to do this work emerged, i.e

... (the) effort to overcome the psychologism in the field of psychotherapy where it usually coexists with a "pathologism." But both are aspects of a more comprehensive phenomenon, namely reductionism, which also includes sociologism and biologism. Reductionism is today's nihilism. It reduces a human being, by no less than an entire dimension. Namely the specific human dimension. It projects what is uniquely human from the three-dimensional plane of the total human being into the two-dimensional plane of the subhuman. In other words, reductionism is subhumanism (Frankl, 1997, pp. 59-60).

It was when I heard these words of Dr. Frankl in 1968 at Baker University that I knew he was explaining something that had a high degree of relevance and veracity. He spoke of the specifically human dimension, the noetic dimension or the dimension of the human spirit. He spoke of how this dimension contained the largest amount of resources that one could bring to bear on the vicissitudes of life. It was through the recognition of the interrelatedness of all three of the dimensions of the human being that the wholeness of the human being could be realized.

In 1968, Dr. Frankl was 63 years old and yet displayed an enormous amount of energy and a genuine appreciation for life. His enthusiasm was contagious. America was in the throws of turmoil, the results of which were not dissimilar to the time of Dr. Frankl's own boyhood. His account was riveting. America, he said, was being cut loose from the bonds of tradition and was beginning to float aimlessly, like a ship without a rudder. In addition to its Statue of Liberty on the east coast, he stated that America needed to have a Statue of Responsibility on the west coast. It was the balance of these two pinions, in his opinion, that kept a society from a meaningless meander through the gates of history.

Dr. Frankl received one of his eventual 29 honorary doctoral degrees from Baker University that year. It was a small gift in comparison to the enormous amount of life-changing information that Dr. Frankl imparted to those of us who were privileged to experience his presence and benefit from his experience and wisdom. Without a doubt, it was the stories of his years of suffering and survival in four concentration camps that captured the attention of the Baker students. Frankl had obviously earned the right to be heard and certainly shared information worth hearing.

Before his life ended, Dr. Frankl had written 32 books that have been published in 32 languages. He lectured at 209 universities on five continents. He held both M.D. and PhD. Degrees and is also the recipient of the Dr.h.c.mult. academic title due to his numerous honorary degrees. *Man's Search for Meaning,* copyrighted in 1959 and first published by Washington Square Press in 1963, sold over five million copies in the United States. The Library of Congress and Book of the Month club survey listed it as one of the ten "most influential books in America" according to a report in 1991.

Viktor Frankl's Logotherapy is recognized as the "third Viennese School of Psychotherapy." Dr. Graber reports, "The American Medical Society, the American Psychiatric Association and the American Psychological Association have officially recognized Dr. Frankl's Logotherapy as one of the scientifically based schools of psychotherapy. According to the American Journal of Psychiatry, his work is 'perhaps the most significant thinking since Freud and Adler'" (Graber, 2004, p. 21). There are over 86 institutes and organizations in 34 countries dedicated to the education, training and practice of Logotherapy. Dr. Frankl published the last two of his 32 books in 1997. They were *Viktor Frankl – Recollections* and *Man's Search for Ultimate Meaning.* He died at the age of 92.

Commitment that Changed Everything

Dr. Frankl's decision to remain in Vienna rather than take advantage of his visa to the United States of America was a decision that altered the course of his life. He asked for and received what he believed to be a "sign" that he should stay in Vienna with his parents. When his father showed him the stone fragment from their synagogue that his father had salvaged after the Nazi's destroyed the building and the letter on the stone was one of the letters in the commandment to "Honor your father and your mother," Frankl accepted that as his sign to stay. This was an act of self-transcendence, which Frankl believed could be demonstrated in life through *meaning fulfillment* or *loving encounter* (Frankl, 1978, p. 35).

William Blair Gould quotes Frankl from his book *The Unheard Cry for Meaning* and then comments further when he writes:

> "self-transcendence . . . is equally implied whether a man transcends himself by *meaning fulfillment* or *loving encounter:* in the first case, an impersonal logos is involved; in the second, a personal logos (a sense of meaning) – an incarnate logos, so to speak." Essentially, Freud symbolizes the impersonal logos with his desire for meaning fulfillment centered in his vocation; Frankl symbolizes a personal logos. Frankl became an incarnate logos of love to his family, to his friends, and when the time came, to his fellow prisoners in the concentration camps. The presence of a personal logos gave Frankl the strength to survive the concentration camps for two and a half years. Self-transcendence helped him to find meaning in significant ways (Gould, 1993, p. 7).

His life was in Vienna. His work was there. His fiancé was there. His love of climbing was there along with the Donauland Alpine Club. He truly cherished his participation in the activities of the club and was close to a great number of its members. One of the immediate and significant losses he experienced upon his arrival at Auschwitz was the badge from the Donauland Alpine Club, which symbolized his certification as a climbing guide.

His own sister had earlier left for Australia where she escaped the Holocaust. Dr. Frankl could have done the same, but had he done so, it is highly unlikely that his development of Logotherapy and the attention that it received worldwide would have been anything near the magnitude that it has enjoyed.

Most of the tenets of Logotherapy were developed in the time between Dr. Frankl's youth and his early career as a psychiatrist, but they were proven in the deepest throws of humanity's ability to be inhumane in the German concentration camps of World War II. It is somewhat ironic that Dr. Freud decided to stay in Vienna due to his poor health and his concerns that, if he left, his fledgling psychoanalytical movement would dissipate. In the end, however, Dr. Freud relented, moved to England, and ended up seeking English citizenship as a final repudiation of his homeland. Dr. Frankl, on the other hand, wished to stay in order to meet what he felt were his obligations to others and, as a result, survived World War II to return to his homeland, where he found true meaning in life. It was in the survival of the rigors of the concentration camps that he discovered just how true the tenets of his Logotherapy actually were.

Concentration Camps

Within nine months after his wedding to his first wife, Tilly Grosser, they were taken to Theresienstadt, a camp that was "less reprehensible than most." They had been married as one of the last two Jewish couples to be married before the closing and dissolution of the Jewish registrar's office. Even though it was not "official," Jewish couples were not allowed to have children. Dr. Frankl writes:

The Medical Society was instructed not to interfere with abortions on Jewish women. Tilly had to sacrifice the fetus she was carrying. My book, *The Unheard Cry for Meaning,* is dedicated to this, our unborn child (Frankl, 1997, p. 87).

Dr. Frankl had been in Theresienstadt only a few days when he:
> . . . got a bitter taste of "a real concentration camp." After a few hours of labor, I was dragged back to my barracks with 31 wounds of varying severity, dragged by a Viennese rascal – a petty criminal . . . On the way back, Tilly saw me and rushed to my side. "For heavens sake, what have they done to you?" In the barrack she, the trained nurse, bandaged me and took care of me. That evening, when I had recovered somewhat, she wanted to divert my attention from my misery. So she took me to another barrack where a jazz band, known in Prague, was playing – without official permission. They played a tune that was the unofficial "national anthem" of the Jews in Theresienstadt: *"Bei mir bist du schon"* ("To me, you are beautiful"). The contrast between the indescribable tortures of the morning and the jazz in the evening was typical of our existence (Frankl, 1997, pp. 92-93).

Little did they realize that the attempt to keep Tilly safe from being transported to Auschwitz would be short-lived. Dr. Frankl was called up for "Transport East" which mostly meant Auschwitz. Even though he tried ardently not to have Tilly volunteer to go in his transport, she could not be persuaded and did volunteer to go with him. As the men and women were being separated, Dr. Frankl's last words to Tilly were, "Tilly, stay alive at any price. Do you hear? At any price!"

His hopes were realized for almost four years, although he never saw her again. He learned upon his own release in August of 1945, that Tilly had died after the liberation of Bergen-Belsen by English soldiers. The soldiers had discovered 17,000 corpses when they liberated the remaining prisoners. During the following six weeks, 17,000 more died from sickness, starvation, and exhaustion. Tilly was among them (Frankl, 1997, pp. 86-91).

Dr. Frankl's arrival at Auschwitz set the stage for the worst time in his life, from which the best he could bring to it and glean from it would mold and test the tenets of his Logotherapy. The results would change the world.

When he arrived at Auschwitz, his hopes were dashed. He had sewn the manuscript of his first book, later to be published as *The Doctor and the Soul*, into the lining of his overcoat. This manuscript, which he had written as the situation in Vienna grew worse, was his attempt to have the essentials of Logotherapy survive him. It, along with all of his clothes, were immediately taken from him and lost forever.

In return for his own perfectly good coat, Dr. Frankl was given the clothing of another who had already been gassed. In the pocket of the coat he found a leaf torn from a prayer book on which was written the *Shema Israel,* the principal prayer of Judaism. It is, "Hear, oh Israel, the Lord our God is One" (Frankl, 1997, pp. 93-94). This "coincidence" was interpreted by Dr. Frankl as a message that he was to live and to practice what he preached in Logotherapy.

He was in line with the others who had just arrived at the camp and proceeded to pass by Dr. Joseph Mengele, the horrible mass murderer of the Holocaust. Dr. Mengele pointed Dr. Frankl's shoulder to the left. As he walked on, he did not notice any of his friends in that group, so Dr. Frankl simply crossed to the other group behind the back of Dr. Mengele. The group on the left went directly to the gas chambers. All of the people in that group were killed that day.

The same Viennese common criminal that had punished Dr. Frankl at Theresienstadt had become a Capo at Auschwitz. The following took place not long after Dr. Frankl's arrival.

> I was the last one to be put into a group of 100 earmarked for transport. Just as our group was about to be moved forward, this rascal pounced on another inmate who was standing nearby and began to beat him with a barrage of body blows. Then he literally kicked the inmate into our group, at the same time grabbing me and pulling me out. He cursed the beaten prisoner with a flood of filthy profanities, and made it appear that he had tried to slip out of the group. By the time I realized what was happening, the 100 men were already being marched off without me. The rascal – my protector, in this case – must have known that the group was ill-fated, perhaps destined for the gas chambers. (Now I am convinced that this scalawag saved my life) (Frankl, 1997, p. 95).

In the third of the four concentration camps that Dr. Frankl survived, Kaufering III, he almost lost his life to what he believed was the number one killer of those who died in the concentration camps outside of the gas chambers, pessimism and depression. Dr. Frankl credits Mr. Benscher, a man who later became a television actor in Munich, with a conversation that woke him up to the seriousness of his situation. Dr. Frankl writes:

> While I was sipping soup, he talked to me with great urgency, imploring me to get over my pessimism. The mood that had overcome me was the mood I had observed in other inmates, which almost inevitably led to giving up and, sooner or later, to death (Frankl, 1997, p. 95).

In Turkheim, Dr. Frankl almost died from typhus. He kept lamenting over the fact that his book would never get published if he died in the camps. Finally he asked himself the question, "What kind of life would it be, whose meaning depends entirely on whether a book gets published" (Frankl, 1997, p. 95)? He remembered his Jewish teachings about Abraham and the sacrifice of his son. He believed that he needed to come to the place where he was willing to sacrifice his book, his "spiritual child" . . . in order to be judged worthy of its eventual publication" (Frankl, 1997, p. 97).

It was in Turkheim that Dr. Frankl crawled on his stomach through the darkness for over 100 yards at the peril of certain death if caught in order to visit Dr. Racz, the head physician of the camp, to be treated for Typhus. His choice was to take this risk or to die from choking.

In each of the four camps, Dr. Frankl learned lessons that upheld his original suppositions about Logotherapy. While he claimed never to have had nightmares about *Matura,* the rigorous final exams in high school that often caused nightmares for many of the Austrian students, he did have nightmares about the concentration camps throughout his life. For Dr. Frankl, his experiences in the concentration camps were his own test of maturation. The camps were,

> . . . the *experimentum cruces.* The two basic human capacities, self-transcendence and self-distancing, were verified and validated in the concentration camps.

This experiential evidence confirms the survival value of "the will to meaning" and the self-transcendence – the reaching out beyond ourselves for something other than ourselves. Under the same conditions, those who were oriented toward the future, toward a meaning that waited to be fulfilled – these persons were more likely to survive. Nardini and Lifton, two American military psychiatrists, found the same to be the case in the prisoner-of-war camps in Japan and Korea (Frankl, 1997, p. 97).

Early Logotherapy Years

Logotherapy was developed in the graciousness of a middle-class, Viennese society. It was tested in the bowels of hell, the German concentration camps of World War II. From the formation through the testing and ultimately to the world since that time, Logotherapy has remained true to its formation. Throughout his years as a student relating to Dr. Freud through letters and Dr. Adler as his one-time prized student, Dr. Frankl developed his theories concerning psychoanalysis and individual psychology which helped in his formation of the theories of Logotherapy.

> As early as 1929 I had developed the concept of three groups of values, or three possible ways to find meaning in life – even up to the last moment, the last breath. The three possibilities are: 1) a deed we do, a work we create; 2) and experience, a human encounter, a love; and 3) when confronted with an unchangeable fate (such as an incurable disease), a change of attitude toward that fate. In such cases we still can wrest meaning from life by giving testimony to the most human of all human capacities: the ability to turn suffering into a human triumph (Frankl, 1997, p. 64).

It was by 1933, during a lecture to the study group of the Academic Society for Medical Psychology in Vienna that Dr. Frankl first used the term *Existenzanalyse (existential analysis)* and called it Logotherapy. He used the term consistently from that time on and stated "By that time I had systematized my ideas to some extent" (Frankl, 1997, p. 64). The systematization of the theories that serve as the foundation of Logotherapy grew from his work with youth counseling centers, which he helped to found, first in Vienna, and then in six other cities. These centers were places where "young people in personal and psychological distress could turn for counseling" (Frankl, 1997, p. 68).

His theories also grew from his work with a wing of suicidal women at the mental hospital, *Am Steinhof*. He claimed that his diagnostic skills were honed a great deal during that time. Dr. Frankl was given permission by the chief of psychotherapy at Potzl Clinic, Otto Kogerer, to begin working at the clinic without supervision because Dr. Frankl was so greatly admired and his involvement in the psychoanalytical movement was so greatly respected. He was, in all respects, a young prodigy in the field.

This trust allowed for a variance that resulted in the further development of his theories.

> I tried to forget what I had learned from psychoanalysis and individual psychology so that I could learn from listening to my patients. I wanted to find out how they managed to improve their conditions. I began to improvise.
>
> I easily remembered what patients told me, but I often forgot what I told them. So it happened repeatedly that I heard from my patients how they had practiced paradoxical intention. When I asked them how they happened to think of such tricks to fight their neuroses, they were surprised and answered: "Why, it was you who told me." I had forgotten my own invention (Frankl, 1997, p. 73).

Latter Logotherapy Years

During the last third of his life, Dr. Frankl became more and more interested in expanding the reach as well as the foundations of Logotherapy. Logotherapy had become a reality on the world stage of psychology. Dr. Frankl lectured at universities on five continents making no less than 92 separate trips to America alone. His early interest in philosophy resulted in two things; first, a PhD in philosophy earned 19 years following his M.D. , and second, the deepening of the foundations of Logotherapy through the development of what Dr. Frankl liked to call Logo philosophy.

Volition is a central tenet of the philosophy of Logotherapy. It was one of the points of argument between the Freudian and Adlerian schools of psychotherapy. Frankl agreed with Adler that volition was part of the human reality and gave volition an even more prominent place in Logotherapy. Dr. Frankl agreed that biology and physical circumstances play a role in the quality of life and the range of decisions that can be made at any given time in a person's life, but stressed that the Freedom of the Will when combined with the Will to Meaning will give people many more options than either of the other two schools granted.

Dr. Frankl's original term for Logotherapy was *Existential Analysis.* Existential thought is based on the reality and nature of human existence and upon the belief that humans create the meaning and essence of their lives. The focus of Existentialism is that humans are absolutely free and, therefore, responsible for their choices and the effect of their choices upon their lives. In Existentialism it is up to humans to create an ethos of personal responsibility aside from any particular system of beliefs.

Existentialism began in the nineteenth century with Soren Kiekegaard and Friedrich Neitzsche being the prominent philosophers. It emerged in the twentieth century as a force in philosophy and literature postulating the absence of a transcendent force of meaning. The absence of this transcendent focus highlights the nature of personal responsibility.

Existential psychology is one of the major offshoots of Existential philosophy. Dr. Frankl was among the preeminent practitioners of this developing psychology. Logotherapy made two distinct contributions. The first was the recognition that even among the distinctly worst circumstances in life, such as his own experiences in the German concentration camps, one can find meaning that is helpful in life in the midst of unalterable suffering. Such transcendence is at the heart of Logotherapy. The second is the strong recognition of the noetic dimension, the dimension that Dr. Frankl calls the distinctly human dimension.

> Frankl also recognizes the paradoxical nature of existence, but he escapes both the piety of Kierkegaard and the secular elitism of Nietzsche by focusing in his search, on meaning. . . . He writes that "in the dimension of the body we are imprisoned; in the dimension of the psyche we are driven; but in the dimension of the spirit we are free" (Gould, 1993, p. 107).

Logotherapy acts upon the assumption that every individual has a Will to Meaning which, when thwarted, causes an existential vaccum that skews decisions and creates serious behavioral problems. In addressing the reality of nihilism in the existential expressions of Mounier, Paschal, and Sartre,

> Frankl feels that psychotherapy may often reflect nihilism, and as a result, the patient is shown a distorted rather than a true image of Being. . . . In contrast to a neurotic, who lives his or her life looking backward, the meaning-oriented person finds significance in the present and believes that meaning will be further fulfilled in the future. Lived nihilism is replaced by lived meaning – finding meaning through a task worth doing or caring for another. The misanthropy of nihilism is replaced by the philanthropy of a life of meaning (Gould, 1993, p. 123).

Phenomenology is another philosophy that met with a warm reception from Dr. Frankl. Although phenomenology was mentioned in a variety of ways as early as the eighteenth century, it was not until the latter part of the century and the early part of the nineteenth century that phenomenology was articulated as a philosophy. G. W. F. Hegel was the person credited with establishing dialectical phenomenology. It was further developed by Edmund Husserl and later by Martin Heidegger.

The direct appeal of phenomenology to Dr. Frankl centered around the recognition in phenomenology of the individual and the rejection of the reductionism of the more exclusively scientific approach. One of the characteristics of phenomenology is the intentionality of consciousness. It states that consciousness is always a result of intentionality. It sees every mental act as relating to an intentional object. It is this intentionality that distinguishes mental/psychological phenomena from physical phenomena or objects.

Dr. Frankl was well grounded in Freudian psychoanalysis and in existential phenomenology. From this depth of knowledge and experience, Dr. Frankl suggested some significant differences.

> Frankl's grounding in classical humanism and his studies of existential phenomenology cause him to reject the psychological self for the fully human self (mind, body, and spirit). In constructing a holistic view of the self, Frankl brings new dynamics and interpretations to existential phenomenology (Gould, 1993, p. 46).

Dr. Frankl categorized Logotherapy as existential and phenomenological. He recognized the Freedom of the Will and the exercise of volition as well as the high value of the individual as key tenets in Logotherapy.

> Freedom of the will belongs to the immediate data of our experience, including the prereflective as well as the reflective. This is important in comparing Frankl with Freud, for while Frankl agrees with Freud that the subconscious self is basic, he calls it the prereflective self and links it to the noetic dimension, rather than to the psychosexual needs. Thus the self is free to rise

above the plane of the somatic and psychic determinants of its existence. . . .A major achievement of Frankl's is his challenge to Freudianism in psychotherapy, behaviorism in psychology, and positivism in philosophy (Gould, 1993, pp. 46-47).

A vital part of the applicability of Logotherapy is its broad foundations in philosophy. Existential Analysis is based on a foundation of existential and phenomenological philosophy including the challenges that Dr. Frankl's thinking brings to the discussion. Dr. Frankl's focus is experiencial and academic rather than primarily academic. For this reason, Logotherapy/Existential Analysis is considered a scientific approach to an active and experiencial therapy.

Principles of Logotherapy

Three vital assumptions of Logotherapy/Existential Analysis are 1) Freedom of the Will, 2) the Will to Meaning, and 3) Meaning of Life. These three assumptions form the foundational tenets of Dr. Frankl's development of Logotherapy/Existential Analysis and Logophilosophy.

Freedom of the Will

The Freedom of the Will is the first of three basic assumptions that defines the foundations of Logotherapy. In his book, *The Will to Meaning,* Dr. Frankl states that "the freedom of will involves the issue of determinism versus pan-determinism" (Frankl, 1969, p.vii). It is the philosophical addressing of the issue of volition as it relates to human actions that relate to the conditions that surround and confront us. Dr. Frankl is clear that his view of freedom of the will in no way implies indeterminism.

> . . . the freedom of will, is opposed to a principle that characterizes most current approaches to man, namely, determinism. Really, however, it is only opposed to what I am used to calling pan-determinism, because

speaking of the freedom of will does not in any way imply any *a priori* indeterminism. After all, the freedom of will means the freedom of human will, and human will is the will of a finite being. Man's freedom is not freedom from conditions but rather freedom to take a stand on whatever conditions might confront him (Frankl, 1969, p. 16).

Freedom of the will allows for biological, psychological, or sociological conditions and their effect upon the freedom of humans. It also recognizes the distinctly human capability of humor and heroism to allow humans to choose a form of self-detachment that allows for self-transcendence. Because of this uniquely human capability, a person can shape their own character and is responsible in large part for what he or she has made of himself or herself. Since we have the power to take a stand toward our drives and instincts, we have the opportunity and the responsibility to shape ourselves in relation to them rather than allow ourselves to be shaped by them.

The question of freedom of choice is muddled by reductionism. It is Dr. Frankl's view that reductionism, be it through biology or psychology, causes humans to be viewed in ways that are not representative of their true ontology. Biology can reduce humans to a series of physiological reflexes. Psychology can reduce humans to psychological reactions and responses to stimuli. However, when either of these reductionistic practices are applied to humans, they become less than human. Humans are open to the world around them and humans exhibit self-transcendence. In fact, the most human of all traits is the understanding that being human is "being directed and pointing to something or someone other than itself" (Frankl, 1969, p. 26).

Now it may also have become understandable why sound findings of research in the lower dimensions, however they may neglect the humanness of man, need not contradict it. This is equally true of approaches as distinct as Watsonian behaviorism, Pavlovian reflexology, Freudian psychoanalysis, and Adlerian psychology. They are not nullified by logotherapy but rather overarched by it. They are seen in the light of a higher dimension – or, as the Norwegian psychotherapist Bjarne Kvilhaug put it with special reference to learning theory and behavior therapy, the findings of these schools are reinterpreted and reevaluated by logotherapy – and rehumanized by it (Frankl, 1969, p. 20).

As a result of his understanding of the multidimensionality of human ontology, Dr. Frankl concludes that both diagnosis and therapy should be multidimensional as well.

Science cannot cope with reality in its multidimensionality but must deal with reality as if reality were unidimensional. However, a scientist should remain aware of what he does, if for no other reason than to avoid the pitfalls of reductionism (Frankl, 1969, p. 30).

Will to Meaning

Human beings are certainly animals, but they are also certainly more than animals. The genus *homo sapiens* is ultimately different from other animals in that human beings reach out to the world in such a way that they finally attain a world replete with "other beings to encounter, and meanings to fulfill" (Frankl, 1969, p. 31). Psychological theories previous to Logotherapy were based on the assumption that the homeostasis principle was the preferred result. This principle states that establishing an inner equilibrium and reaching a reduction of tensions is the normal way for a human being to be psychologically healthy.

Freud's psychoanalysis is based on the assumption that neuroses are the result of repressed feelings that need to be given appropriate expression in order to attain an inner equilibrium and homeostasis. The will to pleasure that accompanies this assumption is key to Freudian psychology. Dr. Frankl shows how this will to pleasure is both reductionistic and self-defeating. The human being has a native orientation toward creating and toward the establishment of values.

> As for the pleasure principle, I would go even further in my criticism. It is my contention that, in the final analysis, the pleasure principle is self-defeating. The more one aims at pleasure, the more his aim is missed. In other words, the very "pursuit of happiness" is what thwarts it. This self-defeating quality of pleasure-seeking accounts for many sexual neuroses. . . .
> Normally pleasure is never the goal of human strivings but rather is, and must remain, an effect, more specifically, the side effect of attaining a goal. Attaining the goal constitutes a reason for being happy. In other words, if there is a reason for happiness, *happiness ensues,* automatically and spontaneously, as it were. And that is why *one need not pursue happiness,* one need not care for it once there is a reason for it (Frankl, 1969, pp. 33-34).

In addition to not needing to be concerned about happiness, Dr. Frankl states that *"one cannot pursue it."* By pursuing it, one will lose sight of the reason for it and thereby lose happiness. Happiness is a by-product of a goal, well-chosen, pursued, and at least somewhat attained. Happiness ensues as a result of these distinctly human activities.

The will to power or the status drive of Adler is also based on a false assumption that homeostasis is the preferred outcome of a psychologically healthy individual. Dr. Frankl states that this, too, is misconceived.

In the final analysis, the status drive or the will to power, on one hand, and the pleasure principle or, as one might term it as well, the will to pleasure, on the other hand, are mere derivatives of man's primary concern, that is, his will to meaning – the second within the triad of concepts on which logotherapy is based. What I call the will to meaning could be defined as the basic striving of man to find and fulfill meaning and purpose.

But what is the justification of calling the will to power and the will to pleasure mere derivatives of the will to meaning? Simply that pleasure, rather than being an end of man's striving, is actually the effect of meaning fulfillment. And power, rather than being an end in itself, is actually the means to an end; if man is to live out his will to meaning, a certain amount of power – say, financial power – by and large will be an indispensable prerequisite. Only if one's original concern with meaning fulfillment is frustrated is one either *content with power* or *intent on pleasure* (Frankl, 1969, p. 35).

Dr. Frankl was clear that one other important difference between his theories and those of Freud and Adler was found in the motivational direction and influence of their theories. For Freud and Adler, the will to pleasure and the will to power were "drives" that pushed humans forward in their thoughts and actions toward homeostasis. Dr. Frankl states that the will to meaning is not a drive that pushes, but rather an attraction that "draws" humans toward their goal of meaning fulfillment and purpose.

The existential approach of Dr. Frankl has put volition and will back in the center of the issue. Intentionality is primary in this approach and that intentionality demands a freedom of the will that allows for the will to meaning. It is also important to distinguish between the will to meaning and simple "will-power" or voluntarism. It is not possible for a person to "will to will" or to demand, command, or order the will to meaning. As Dr. Frankl states, ". . . if the will to meaning is to be elicited, meaning itself has to be elucidated (Frankl, 1969, p. 44).

The largest frustration to the will to meaning in modern American society is the lack of tension experienced in an affluent society. The error of the homeostatic principle is that it fails to recognize that human beings require a healthy tension in order to avoid an existential vacuum. This existential vacuum is the frustration of the will to meaning. The presence of a meaning to fulfill creates a healthy tension that produces a focus that transcends the self and grants a true purpose in life. Without this healthy tension, human beings will create tension, often in unhealthy ways resulting in the deterioration of society rather than its betterment.

Meaning in Life
The third foundation of Logotherapy is found in the assumption that there is meaning in life. This assumption is undergirded with the existential understanding that not only is existence intentional, but it is also transcendent. For Dr. Frankl and those who ascribe to the tenets of Logotherapy and Logophilosophy, self-transcendence is the essence of existence. The question of meaning in life is the questions of objectivity and subjectivity.

Dr. Frankl addresses this issue in a straightforward manner:
> Those authors who pretend to have overcome the dichotomy between object and subject are not aware that, as a truly phenomenological analysis would reveal, there is no such thing as cognition outside of the polar field of tension established between object and subject. These authors are used to speaking of "being in the world." Yet to understand this phrase

properly, one must recognize that being human profoundly means being engaged and entangled in a situation, and confronted with a world whose objectivity and reality is in no way detracted from by the subjectivity of that "being" who is "in the world." Preserving the "otherness," the objective-ness, of the object means preserving that tension which is established between object and subject. This tension is the same as the tension between the "I am" and the "I ought," between reality and ideal, between being and meaning. And if this tension is to be preserved, meaning has to be prevented from coinciding with being. *I should say that it is the meaning of meaning to set the pace of being* (Frankl, 1969, pp. 50-51) (Italics are mine).

Human beings live best when they recognize the inherent tension between reality and ideals to materialize. We live by ideals and values. When we overemphasize subjectivity and relativism, we devalue and threaten the existence of self-transcendence. The battle in life becomes a battle for meaning over against an existential vacuum that occurs when meaning is absent or trivialized. Experience says that we can not do either for life dictates differently.

According to one definition, meanings and values are nothing but reaction formations and defense mechanisms. As for myself, I would not be willing to live for the sake of my reaction formations, even less to die for the sake of my defense mechanisms (Frankl, 1969, p. 54).

For the most part, meanings are unique. They are unique to the person and unique to the moment. While there is no universal meaning of life, there are meanings which are shared among people. These shared meanings cross sociological and historical divisions. These shared meanings are what are known as values. While this sharing of meanings lessens the probability of existential vacuum, the cost is the perception of the collision of values and the possibility of what Dr. Frankl has termed noogenic neuroses.

Dr. Frankl describes the difference between unique meanings and values as well as the hierarchical relationship of values in this way:

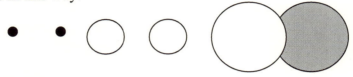

Figure 1

Let us imagine that unique meanings are points, while values are circles. It is understandable that two values may overlap with one another, whereas this cannot happen to unique meanings. But we must ask ourselves whether two values can really collide with one another, in other words, whether their analogy with two-dimensional circles is correct. Would it not be more correct to compare values with three-dimensional spheres? Two three-dimensional spheres projected out of the three-dimensional space down into the two-dimensional plane may well yield two two-dimensional circles overlapping one another, although the spheres themselves do not even touch on one another. The impression that two values collide with one another is a consequence of the fact that a whole dimension is disregarded. And what is this dimension? It is the hierarchical order of values. According to Max Scheler, valuing implicitly means preferring one value to another. This is the final result of his profound phenominological analysis of valuing processes. The rank of a value is experienced together with the value itself. In other words, the experience of one value includes the experience that it ranks higher than another. There is no place for value conflicts.

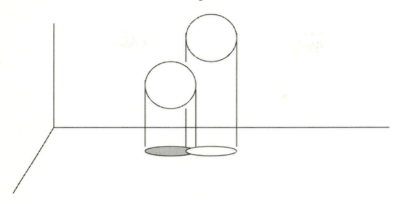

Figure 2

However, the experience of the hierarchical order of values does not dispense man from decision-making. Man is pushed by drives. But he is pulled by values. He is always free to accept or to reject a value he is offered by a situation. This is also true of the hierarchical order of values as it is channeled by moral and ethical traditions and standards. They still have to stand a test, the test of man's conscience – unless he refuses to obey his conscience and suppresses its voice (Frankl, 1969, pp. 56-57).

Another component of this foundational tenet of Logotherapy is what Dr. Frankl calls the "demand quality of life." Meaning is realized in its uniqueness in various settings, each of which add to the demand quality that life brings to all who live it. The person brings their own uniqueness to life which shapes the meaning of the moment. Each moment in life is unique and brings a unique set of meanings to be fulfilled. Finally, the truly self-transcendent quality of human life causes us to reach out for something other than ourselves in order to experience true meaning fulfillment.

These three qualities that are each unique in themselves cause us to experience the true demand quality of life. It is life that brings these unique possibilities together and presents us consistently with meanings to be fulfilled. Our choices determine our willingness to participate in the process of meaning fulfillment or to avoid it and experience the types of noogenic neuroses that can result for the existential vacuum created by those very choices. This demand quality of life is the call to be human by being responsible and self-transcendent. It is the essence of the search for meaning.

In addition to these meanings of the moment, there is also a demand quality given to life by ultimate meanings (Gould, 1993, p. 57). Dr. Frankl explains this in terms of the relationship of the various human dimensions.

> A higher dimension, by definition, is a more *inclusive* one. The lower dimension is included in the higher one; it is subsumed in it and encompassed by it. Thus biology is overarched by psychology, psychology by noology, and noology by theology.
>
> The noological dimension may rightly be defined as the dimension of uniquely human phenomena. Among them, there is one which I regard as the most representative of the human reality. I have circumscribed this phenomenon in terms of "man's search for meaning." Now if this is correct, one may also be justified in defining religion as man's search for *ultimate* meaning (Frankl, 1975, p. 13).

Ultimate meaning opens to the dimension of that which subsumes all that is comprehensible and transcends it. It can be glimpsed as all of the meanings of the moment experienced in life that add up to a larger and more meaningful understanding of life by being able to look back over those meanings of the moment at the end of one's life and understanding, by doing so, a greater, deeper sense of meaning. But even this is just a glimpse as it incorporates only those meanings of the moment that were actualized in one single life. Ultimate meaning includes all of those meanings of the moment for all of the lives that have ever existed and yet transcends them.

But once we start dealing with an overall meaning we soon meet a law that I would like to formulate as follows: *The more comprehensive the meaning, the less comprehesible it is.* And if it comes to *ultimate meaning*, also, it necessarily is beyond comprehension (Frankl, 1997, MSUM, p. 143).

In personal conversation with Dr. Frankl during an Introduction to Religion class at Baker University in the late 1960's, I asked Dr. Frankl why he did not just call ultimate meaning "God." His answer was quite a surprise and quite revealing. He stated that there was a domain for psychology and a domain for religion and at some very important points they overlapped each other, but as a psychiatrist and Logotherapist he needed to remain in the domain of psychology if Logotherapy was to be taken seriously in the world of science. There was, he said, a very definite place in philosophy for the tenets of Logotherapy and when correctly understood, the overlap between psychology and religion could be better understood through Logotherapy. He also stated that while he had a great interest in this area, he did not have the time to pursue it and would have to leave that up to "people like you."

I knew from the wry smile on his face he was using that phrase in a generic way, inferring that those with a deep enough interest in the fields of religion and Logotherapy could take the time to address that question. I will admit that I saw that moment as an open door and an invitation to become such a person.

Later in his life, Dr. Frankl did take time to elaborate about ultimate meaning and its relationship to religion.

I admit that the concept of religion in its widest possible sense as it is here propounded goes far beyond the narrow concepts of God as they are promulgated by some representatives of denominational religion. They often depict, not to say denigrate, God as a being who is primarily concerned with being believed in by the greatest possible number of believers and along the lines of a specific creed, at that. "Just believe," we are told, "and everything will be okay." But alas, not only is this order based on a distortion of any sound concept of deity, but even more important, it is doomed to failure: Obviously, there are certain activities that simply cannot be commanded, demanded, or ordered. You cannot order anyone to laugh – if you want him to laugh, you must tell him a joke. And if you want people to have faith and belief in God, you cannot rely on preaching along the lines of a particular church but must, in the first place, portray your God believably - and you must act credibly yourself. In other words, you have to do the very opposite of what so often is done by the representatives of organized religion when they build up an image of God as someone who is primarily interested in being believed in and who rigorously insists that those who believe in him be affiliated with a particular church. Small wonder that such representatives of religion behave as though they saw the main task of their own denomination as that of overriding other denominations (Frankl, 1997, MSUM, p. 150).

Dr. Frankl quoted both Albert Einstein and Ludwig Wittgenstein who, ten years apart from one another, gave very similar definitions of their understandings of religion by saying "To be religious is to have found an answer to the question, What is the meaning of life?" (Einstein) and "To believe in

God is to see that life has a meaning" (Wittgenstein). Frankl concludes his book on ultimate meaning by writing:

> To be sure, there is a question to be left open or, better to say, to be answered by the theologian, namely the question: To which extent are the three definitions of religion acceptable to him? The only thing we psychiatrists can do is to keep the dialogue between religion and psychiatry going; going on in the spirit of that mutual tolerance which is indispensable in the era of pluralism and in the area of medicine; . . . (Frankl, 1997, MSUM, p. 154).

To be certain, Dr. Frankl has shown a definite connection between the "meaning orientation" of Logotherapy and the "ultimate meaning" of religion or theology. He has opened the door to the investigation of how each can contribute to the other through open and tolerant dialogue and through further conjecture and research. It continues to be my contention that by combining an understanding of Franklian psychology and Logophilosophy with a knowledge of "The Three Ways" of Christian spiritual formation, anyone can develop a better understanding of the critical transitions in the Christian spiritual life.

Inclusion of the Noetic Dimension: Greek Roots

Dr. Graber clearly portrays Dr. Frankl's interaction with the Greek philosophers from the beginnings of his classical education. Socrates was quite influential and quite controversial in his time. He had a great influence in Western thought by redirecting the "focus of philosophy from considerations about the origin of the universe to what he considered the most important things: developing moral character, and the search for knowledge that would lead to justice" (Graber, 2004, pp. 23-26).

Dr. Frankl's admiration for Socrates can be seen in his play, *Synchronization in Birkenwald,* as he casts Socrates as the character who:

> is portrayed as the unassuming, patient, elder member among the philosophers who are synchronizing polarities of good and evil, love and hate, time and space through transformative influences to bring about meaningful change in the world (Graber, 2004, p. 25).

Plato, the most famous student of Socrates, further developed Greek thought. His political philosophy and ethics flowed from his understanding of the human soul. The Greek word for soul *psyuche*, actually translates into the soul-life of a human being. It represents that integration of separate, but interdependent dimensions that together form the working of the soul and are known as life. For Plato, this was a tripartite understanding; i.e., the mind (rational and intellectual), the spirit (will), and the body (appetite or desire). This understanding included for Plato the fact that the human being was powered by love *(eros)* which moved from the lower things (the physical) to the higher things (honor and wisdom) as the human being matured philosophically. This tripartite understanding was significantly different from the bipartite understanding of body and soul that was predominant in Roman and early Christian thought.

Dr. Frankl would have been more than familiar with the Greek philosophers. His classical education was based on the metaphysics of Plato and the epistemology of Aristotle. "Plato's description of the ideal state or society in his *Republic* with its three types of citizens, is analogous to the well-functioning soul. Frankl certainly would have been familiar with Plato's metaphysics" (Graber, 2004, p. 26). Dr. Frankl differed with Plato significantly over the motivation of creativity in the human life. While Plato relegated creative motivation to something akin to divine madness, Frankl highly valued creativity. In fact, Dr. Frankl saw creativity as one of the three main ways to discover meaning in life. While Plato thought that the arts should be censored, Frankl encouraged this means of meaning discovery and established Logotherapy on creativity as one of the three methods of meaning discovery. This is just one more example of Dr. Frankl's contention that even a dwarf (*Zwerg*) can see further than a giant when he stands on the giant's sholders. The process of development be it in philosophy, psychology, or theology is often the process of taking that which is made clearer by those who have gone before us and building on those portions of it with which we agree while critiquing, disputing, and even discarding those portions with which we disagree.

Aristotle added a significant component to philosophical thought for Dr. Frankl and those who adhere to Logotherapy. That component was an adherence to practical reason or common sense. Composed of three elements that are separate but interrelated, this model of *phronesis* is made up of theory *(theoria),* action *(praxis),* and production *(poiesis).*

Another point of disagreement with Plato and agreement with Aristotle by Dr. Frankl is that both,

> Aristotle and Frankl, recognize that *perfect* good is humanly unattainable. Frankl follows Aristotle by adopting moderation as the standard of duty for the soul (psyche) in order to achieve a *proportional* goal. As a result, the healthy or happy life is measured by each person's needs, place, and condition. Frankl locates such practical wisdom in what he calls the noological dimension, which he defines as "that dimension in which the specifically human phenomena are located." In contrast, Freud rejects any spiritual dimension in life as deceiving at worst and overprotective at best. He believes that religion must go, for "man cannot remain a child forever; he must venture at last into the hostile world. This may be

called *'education to reality.'* This concept of education to reality is used in different ways by Aristotle and Frankl. Aristotle while recognizing that hostile forces exist in the world believes that the noos allows the greatest good to be realized in this life. For him, education to reality is education to pragmatic truth, which has many dimensions that depend on the individual, his or her location, and the individual's interpretation (either as speaker or hearer) of what is meant by truth and goodness. Like Aristotle, Frankl expands the meaning of the Greek *noos* (mind) to include everything that is human and to provide a holistic understanding that avoids the unfocused mysticism of Plato and the reductionistic materialism of Freud. Frankl's Aristotelianism realizes that the validity of the noos must be tested by logic and experience (Gould, 1993, p. 32).

Dr. Frankl's use of the terms *logos* and *noos,* both of which are Greek terms, also shows his attachment to Greek thinking and expression. His expansion of the term *noos* to include those particular ways that the human mind relate us to responsibility and the demand quality of life is what undergirds the recognition of the noetic realities that human beings experience. The inclusion of the noological dimension is the "rehumanizing" of psychological therapy. It was Frankl's concern with the suffering of people that caused him to demand a recognition of the *homo patiens* (the suffering human being) alongside of the *homo sapiens* (the knowing or wise human being). The ability of the human being to choose the way in which he or she would face the reality of unalterable suffering was proof of the noetic or noological dimension for Frankl. It was as important to the understanding of the reality and nature of the human being as the ability of the human to think and reason. It was the spiritual dimension of the human being; *the dimension of meaning.*

The Greek term *logos,* from which Logotherapy is derived, literally means "word" in the Greek language. A word is a collection of letters that carries a "meaning" or rational understanding from which thoughts are constructed. Without meaning, a word is not a word, it is jibberish. This is why when shown a collection of letters, or in the Cherokee language, a collection of syllables from the syllabry, a person unfamiliar with the meaning of the symbols will not perceive a word, for there is no meaning connected with it. "ii" means nothing to the non-Cherokee speaker even though it means "yes" to the person who knows that language. The true meaning of the word "word" is "meaning." This is why Logotherapy is known as "meaning centered" therapy.

For Plato, *logos* was primarily found as idea or form. For Aristotle, it was more akin to reason or judgment. Heidegger followed the phenomenological axiom to go "back to the things themselves" and understood *logos* to be speech or that which enables language.

Frankl also sees the need for logos, but his understanding of logos goes far beyond the limit set by Heidegger. Frankl builds on Karl Buhler's threefold function of language: "First, language allows the speaker to express himself – it serves as a vehicle of expression. Second, language is an appeal addressed by the speaker to the person to whom he speaks. And third, language always represents something, that 'something' of which one speaks." Heidegger disregards this third function of language while Frankl finds it crucial. To deal with this third function of language, Brentano and Husserl use the term *intentional referent.* As Frankl explains, "All the potential intentional referents together, all those objects which are 'meant' by two subjects communicating with one another, form a structured whole, a world of 'meaning,' and this 'cosmos' of meanings is what may aptly be called the 'logos'" (Gould, 1993, p. 95).

The Noetic Unconscious

The inclusion of the noetic dimension is the primary change in psychotherapy initiated by Dr. Frankl. He often states that Logotherapy is to be a supplemental psychotherapy. This addition of the noetic dimension also expands the understanding of the wholeness of the human being.

> Previously we have tried to supplement psychotherapy in the strict sense of the word by introducing logotherapy as a psychotherapy centered and focusing on the spiritual – which constitutes the noological dimension as distinct from the psychological dimension. Having thus included the spiritual into psychology in general, we now include it in particular into depth psychology – that is, into the psychology of the unconscious (Frankl 1997, MSUM, p. 31).

The noetic dimension is the specifically human dimension. It is the spiritual dimension of the human being. It is in this dimension that one is free to choose. It is in this dimension that one chooses to be responsible. The addition of the noetic dimension alters the perception of depth psychology. Dr. Frankl states it this way.

> Since the instinctual and the spiritual are both unconscious, and the spiritual may be conscious as well as unconscious, we now have to ask ourselves how sharp these two distinctions are. . . .
>
> In contrast to the "fluid" border between the conscious and the unconscious, the line between the spiritual and the instinctual cannot be drawn sharply enough. This fact has been expressed most concisely by Ludwig Binswanger when he spoke of "instincts and spirit" as "incommensurable concepts." Since human existence is spiritual existence, we now see that the distinction

between conscious and unconscious becomes unimportant compared with another distinction: The real criterion of authentically human existence derives from discerning whether a given phenomenon is spiritual or instinctual, whereas it is relatively irrelevant whether it is conscious or unconscious. This is due to the fact that – in contrast to the psychoanalytic concept – being human is not being driven by "deciding what one is going to be," to quote Jaspers *(entscheidendes Sein),* or to quote Heidegger: *Dasein.* I would say that being human is being responsible – existentially responsible, responsible for one's own existence (Frankl, 1997, MSUM, pp. 31-32).

Dr. Frankl "sees the noetic part of the unconscious as a region in which we are not an ego driven by an id but a self, a person relating to others as human beings to be loved and understood rather than things to be used and manipulated" (Graber, 2004, p. 77). It is in the noetic unconscious that we truly find what it is to be human. It is here that we discover the tremendous resources for mental and spiritual health and wholeness. The noetic unconscious is referred to as the storehouse of resources for the human spirit.

Dr. Graber lists the following as a very important portion of the resources found there.
- Our will to meaning
- Our goals and purposes in life
- Our creativity
- Our capacity to love (beyond the physical)
- Our consciousness
- Our sense of humor
- Our commitment to tasks
- Our ideas and ideals
- Our imagination

- Our responsibility and response-ability
- Our self-awareness
- Our compassion
- Our ability to forgive
- Our awareness of mortality (Graber, 2004, p. 78).

Humans are most authentic when they are deciding for themselves rather than being driven by an id. It is in this process of deciding that human beings become conscious of the demand qualities of life and exercise volition, one of the most human of all traits. The presence of the noetic unconscious allows the self to be truly authentic and human rather than animalistic. The noetic dimension is the uniquely human dimension. It is the human spiritual dimension allowing the human being to exercise self-awareness and volition at a larger level than any other species. It is in the noetic unconscious that human beings perceive the voice of meaning.

The Intuitive Conscience

Dr. Frankl states that two of the most human manifestations of the capacity of self-transcendence are love and conscience (Frankl, 1997, MUSM, p. 18). Dr. Graber states that "Since a generalized meaning cannot possible be given to the myriad of situations and experiences in each unique life, an intuitive capacity such as conscience is the only means for grasping the meaning of any moment." The intuitive conscience is that which guides us through the maze of meaningful possibilities in each moment. It is the intuitive conscience that registers the demand quality inherent in each moment of life, those "thousands of commandments arising from the thousands of unique situations of which life consists" (Graber, 2004, p. 79).

The role of self-transcendence is key to understanding what it means to be fully human. The intuitive conscience is the key element of self-transcendence and as such, needs to be both understood and reflected upon. The intuitive conscience can lead us to meaning, but it can also lead us astray. Dr. Frankl's understanding of the intuitive conscious enables us to avoid the rigidity of a structured imperative and the constriction of a reductionistic and moralistic view of life by focusing not only on what is but also on what ought to be.

Storehouse of the Self

Since each individual is unique and lives in the midst of experiences in life that are also unique, being related to time and the constraining circumstances surrounding the myriad of experiences in life, the self becomes a true storehouse of memories and experiences that offer resources for self-transcendence and self-distancing. Self-transcendence and self-distancing are key components of Logotherapy and Logo philosophy. Dr. Frankl was fond of saying that even though restrictions and suffering, such as those he experienced in the concentration camps, can be placed on individuals and their freedoms can be greatly restrained, no one can take away our freedom to choose how we will face such circumstances nor our memories of the meaningful experiences we have had in our lives.

Taking a stand against unavoidable suffering is one of the opportunities afforded human beings because they have a noetic dimension. These human experiences can be extremely helpful in doing more than surviving the rigors of life. Storing these experiences and recalling them during times of unavoidable suffering can help in transcending self and distancing one's self from the suffering.

During his ordeals in one of the four German concentration camps that Dr. Frankl endured, he chose to picture himself in a large lecture hall delivering lectures to students who were very interested in hearing about Logotherapy. Such self-distancing helped him transcend the suffering of the concentration camp. Other prisoners made similar decisions by playing music, remembering pleasant days with relatives and friends, and visioning the future of a life free from the restraints and sufferings that they were enduring.

This process of self-transcendence and self-distancing is possible because the human mind can become a storehouse of the self. Many things can be taken from an individual, but only through biomechanical manipulation or certain serious illnesses can a person be stripped of his or her memories. Because our memories are ours to store, we can call upon them in times of need and find them to be a comfort and strength. Through our memories we can, if we choose, distance ourselves from unavoidable unpleasantness and envision another experience that becomes a reality for us in the process of our imagining it.

The grief that follows the loss of a loved one is another example of the use of the storehouse of the self. By remembering the good, pleasant, and meaningful times spent together, the pain of grief is often lessened and the adjustment to reality without the presence of the loved one is moved forward. This is another benefit of the noetic dimension.

The inclusion of the noetic dimension in Logotherapy is a significant move forward for the discipline of psychology. Previous to Dr. Frankl, the reality of the presence of the noos had been the province of those philosophers that believed in a dimension of human activity that included volitional thought and freedom of choice rather than the closed system of actions that were predetermined by cause and effect for the biological sciences and by divine decree for much of theology. Dr. Frankl brought the third and specifically human dimension into prime consideration in the field of psychology.

CHAPTER III
FRANKLIAN DIMENSIONAL ONTOLOGY

In his discussion of determinism and humanism and his critique of pan-determinism, Dr. Frankl lays the foundation for his understanding of dimensional ontology. He explains that there are three dynamic and interrelated dimensions in the human being. This is in opposition to those who held to the bi-partite theory of the human being, believing that a human being consists of body and soul, or body and mind. Dr. Frankl is adamant in his stating that the human being consists of body (soma), mind (psyche), and spirit (noos). This tri-partite nature of the human being is fundamental to understanding Logotherapy.

This understanding of the human being is essential for the avoidance of pan-determinism and reductionism. By reducing a human being to his or her lowest common denominator one only obtains the portion of the human being that is defined by the dimension into which one is peering. This will never produce a picture of the whole human being and will inevitably lead to a partial view of humankind at best, and a false view of humankind at worst.

Tri-partite Nature of Human Dimensional Ontology

One of Dr. Frankl's favorite stories which addresses the illogical nature of reductionism is as follows:

. . . a rabbi was consulted by two parishioners. One contended that the other's cat had stolen and eaten five pounds of butter, which the other denied. "Bring me the cat," the rabbi ordered. They brought him the cat. "Now bring me scales." They brought him scales. "How many pounds of butter did you say the cat has eaten?" he asked. "Five pounds, rabbi," was the answer. Thereupon the rabbi put the cat on the scales and it weighed exactly five pounds. "Now I have the butter," the rabbi said, "but where is the cat?" This is what happens when eventually the reductionists rediscover in man all the conditioned reflexes, conditioning processes, innate releasing mechanisms and whatever else they have been seeking. "Now we have it," they say, like the rabbi, "but where is the man" (Frankl, 1978, p. 56)?

Somatic Dimension

Human beings consist of three dynamic, interdependent and interrelated dimensions. The first of those dimensions is the somatic dimension, the dimension of the material stuff that gives us a presence in the universe of material objects. It is the dimension of the body. It is dynamic in that it is alive. It changes. Ultimately, it dies or ceases to have life and eventually decays or changes back to its most basic materials. It is interdependent in that without the most basic activity of the brain, the body ceases to have life and function in the material world. It is interrelated in that it is somewhat inseparable from the operation of the brain, an operation that we call mind (mental). We can take the material that makes up the brain and put it in a container and say that we have a brain in our hands, but without the brain functioning, there is no way that the body can have life. The -functioning of the brain is termed the mind even though the phrase "brain function" does not in and of itself fully describe what is meant by the term "mind."

Psychic Dimension

The second dimension of the human being is the psychic or mental/emotional dimension. This dimension consists of the activity of the mind. It is the main focus of the discipline of psychology and psychiatry. This dimension is dynamic in that mental/emotional processes have a reality of their own and, in a sense, a life of their own. The discipline of psychology deals with the arena of normality or abnormality of thought processes and their results. It also deals with the area of psychosomatic realities in both normal and abnormal manifestations. This dimension is interdependent in that it requires the somatic to be present with other realities in the material world. In order to be shared with any other person or the material world, thoughts need to have somatic reality, i.e. a voice, a picture, a gesture, a language, etc. This dimension is interrelated in that both its receiving of data and its imparting of data requires a somatic reality from which it can interpret symbols or sounds which carry meaning.

Noetic Dimension

The third dimension of the human being is the noetic or spiritual dimension. It is the dimension of meaning discovery. It is the specifically human dimension. In this dimension human beings find the freedom to make choices, the volition to will an act and the ability to take a stand against unavoidable suffering. In all of these ways, human beings are elevated above other forms of animal life. In no way does this invalidate the value of other animal life. As one who has grown up working on the farm with animals of all types, I am keenly aware of the perceived ability of animals to communicate in both pleasure and pain, and to think in terms of a response to various stimuli such as fear or hunger. This does not, however, elevate other animal forms to the level of human behavior. As I once said to a class of graduate students I was teaching at Baker University's School of Professional and Graduate Studies, "I will elevate other forms of animal life to the level of human life when I read the first novel written by a porpoise." Until then, I will continue to recognize the sizable difference that exists in animal life forms between human and other forms of animal life.

The noetic dimension is dynamic in that meaning discovery is an ongoing and purposeful part of human life. It is interdependent in that meaning can be discovered throughout the spectrum of the human dimensions. Meaning can be discovered through physical means, through mental/emotional means, and, by its very nature, through noetic or spiritual means. It is interrelated in that the reality of each dimension is not found in its existence but in the way that it relates to meaning discovery and participates in the fulfillment of purpose in life.

Transcendent Nature of Human Dimensional Ontology
It is in this sector of Franklian thought that the development of Logotherapy continues to expand. It is here that I would offer a personal critique and attempt to expand Dr. Frankl's thoughts to what I believe is a more consistent and holistically understandable representation of Dr. Frankl's developing intent. It is here that I would wish to apply Dr. Frankl's own maxim that even a dwarf can see further down the road than a giant when the midget stands on the giant's shoulders.

Dr. Frankl's developing thought about the transcendence and interrelatedness of the human dimensions is seen when one compares his visual analogies and what they represent. In 1969 when he published *The Will to Meaning*, Dr. Frankl represented dimensional ontology with the visualization of the cylinder, the square and the circle as follows.

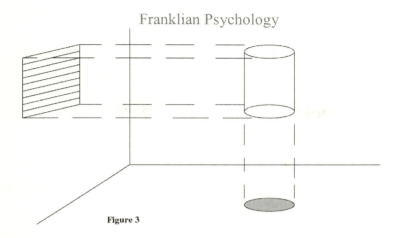

Figure 3

Dr. Frankl explains the figure this way:
Dimensional ontology as I have propounded it, rests on two laws. The first law of dimensional ontology reads: One and the same phenomenon projected out of its own dimension into different dimensions lower than its own is depicted in such a way that the individual pictures contradict one another.
Imagine a cylinder, say, a cup. Projected out of its three-dimensional space into the horizontal and vertical two-dimensional planes, it yields in the first case a circle and in the second one a rectangle. These pictures contradict one another. What is even more important, the cup is an open vessel in contrast to the circle and the rectangle which are closed figures. Another contradiction!
Now let us proceed to the second law of dimensional ontology which reads: Different phenomena projected out of their own dimension into one dimension lower than their own are depicted in such a manner that the pictures are ambiguous.

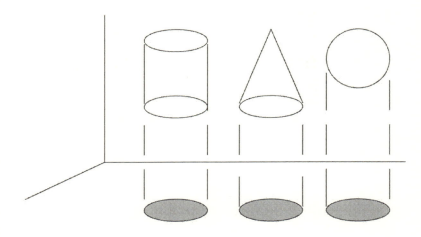

Figure 4

Imagine a cylinder, a cone, and a sphere. The shadows they cast upon the horizontal plane depict them as three circles, which are interchangeable. We cannot infer from a shadow what casts it, what is above it, whether a cylinder, a cone, or a sphere.
According to the first law of dimensional ontology, the projection of a phenomenon into different lower dimensions results in inconsistencies, and according to the second law of dimensional ontology, the projection of different phenomena into a lower dimension results in isomorphies (Frankl, 1969, pp. 23-24).

In 1975, Dr. Frankl sought to explain the spiritual unconscious in relationship to human dimensional ontology via an expansion of his previous visual images. In this expanded version of human dimensional ontology, he explains the image of wholeness that these dimensions seek to exhibit. Dr. Graber has captured the intent of this expansion exceptionally well in her work. She explains it in this way.

A further attempt at conceptualizing and graphically portraying human consciousness is made by Frankl. He depicts the noetic dimension as the innermost core in an ontological model of awareness that is spirit-centered and all inclusive (Fig. 5 *to follow – italics mine*). First Frankl shows the prevalent concept of strata of consciousness ranging from: conscious, preconscious, and unconscious. Then he depicts the model of *layers* of concentric circles of awareness, as propounded by Max Scheler: somatic, psychic, and noetic or spiritual.

By integrating the *strata* model and the *layer* model of concentric circles, Frankl devises a model of *wholeness* that is centered around a spiritual core. This spiritual/noetic axis then would extend, together with the peripheral layers encompassing it, throughout the unconscious, preconscious, and conscious stratum of awareness. Wholeness in this context means integration of the somatic, psychic, and spiritual/noetic dimensions. Only this threefold wholeness makes the human being complete (Graber, 2004, p. 74).

Randy L. Scraper

The following diagram appears in Dr. Graber's book.
WHOLENESS MODEL OF INTEGRATED DIMENSIONS

(based on Frankl, 1975/1985, UG, p. 29)

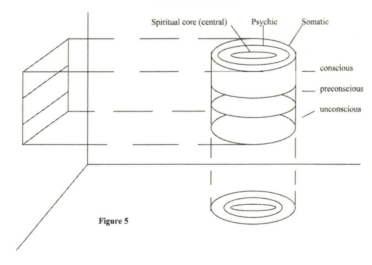

Figure 5

Dr. Frankl continues to explain the integration of human ontological dimensions in 1978. He writes,

> Being centered around the existential, personal, spiritual core, human being is not only individualized but also integrated. Thus the spiritual core, and only

the spiritual core, warrants and constitutes oneness and wholeness in man. Wholeness in this context means the integration of somatic, psychic and spiritual aspects. It is not possible to stress enough that it is only this threefold wholeness which makes man complete. (Frankl, 1978, p. 28).

Dr. Frankl appears to contradict himself, but in fact, further explains himself and shows the developmental nature of his thinking as he seeks to further define dimensional ontology. As seen in figures 3 and 4, objects that are transposed to a lower dimension appear to be contradictory to their actuality. Dr. Frankl states it this way,

> Once we have projected man into the biological and psychological dimensions we also obtain contradictory results. For in one case a biological organism is the result; in the other one, a psychological mechanism. But, however the bodily and mental aspects of human existence might contradict one another, seen in the light of dimensional anthropology this contradiction no longer contradicts the oneness of man. . . .
>
> Because of the self-transcendent quality of human existence, I would say, being human always means being directed and pointing to something or someone other than itself.
>
> All this disappears in the biological and psychological dimensions. But in the light of dimensional anthropology we can at least understand why this must happen. Now the apparent closedness of man in the biological and psychological dimensions no longer contradicts the humanness of man. Closedness in the lower dimensions is very compatible with openness in a higher one, be it the openness of a cylindrical cup, or that of a human being.
>
> Now it may also have become understandable why sound findings of research in the lower dimensions,

however they may neglect the humanness of man, need not contradict it. This is equally true of approaches as distinct as Watsonian behaviorism, Pavlovian reflexology, Freudian psychoanalysis, and Adlerian psychology. They are not nullified by logotherapy but rather overarched by it. They are seen in the light of a higher dimension – or, as the Norwegian psychotherapist Bjarne Kvilhaug put it with special reference to learning theory and behavior therapy, the findings of these schools are reinterpreted and reevaluated by logotherapy – and rehumanized by it.
In this context a warning remark is necessary. Speaking of higher as opposed to lower dimensions does not imply a value judgment. A "higher" dimension just means a more inclusive and encompassing dimension.[5]

(Footnote referenced by Dr. Frankl.)
[5] I well remember how insistent and inquisitive the late Paul Tillich was in the question-and-answer period following my presentation of dimensional ontology at a faculty luncheon of Harvard's Divinity School. He was satisfied only after I had defined the higher dimension as a more inclusive one (Frankl, 1969, pp. 25-26).

    The problem that I detected early in my study of Dr. Frankl's Logotherapy was centered in this developing understanding of dimensional ontology. It became clearer to me upon reading the preceding footnote referencing Paul Tillich's concern. The direct insinuation in Dr. Frankl's writing and visualizations is that the noetic or spiritual dimension is the highest of the human dimensions therefore being the largest and most inclusive of the human dimensions. In Figures 3 and 4, it is clear that the three dimensional object, the cylinder, the cone, or the ball is to be considered as the noetic reality of the human being and that the projections on to a lower plane which are viewed as a rectangle or circle are the somatic or psychic dimension representations.

This analogy breaks down when trying to explain the wholeness of the human being in relation to the conscious, subconscious, and unconscious. Dr. Frankl uses a cylinder in which the "highest" dimension, the noetic or spiritual dimension, is represented by a cylindrical core, wrapped around by the psychological and biological layers as concentric to the noetic or spiritual core. While this represents the "core" nature of the noetic dimension that is essential to Franklian thought, it forces one to recognize that what should be considered the higher and more inclusive dimension, the noetic or spiritual (core) dimension, is seen as a smaller and less inclusive dimension.

While it could be argued that the holistic representation of the human being is the larger dimension in total, it still begs the question that was stated by Dr. Frankl and was the primary concern of Paul Tillich, i.e. the noetic or spiritual dimension of the human being is the highest and therefore the most inclusive of the human dimensions. It is, at its essence, the definition of what a human being is. The biological and psychological overlays are something that a human being has, but the noetic or spiritual core is what a human being is.

I would offer the following figures as visualizations of objects that would more systemically relate the meaning of dimensional ontology while retaining the elements that are essential to Franklian thought. The physics are a bit more involved but understandable.

The representation of the human being with all of his or her dynamic and interdependent dimensions would be a sphere or a ball. One ball for each of the three dimensions. The smallest of the balls would be the somatic dimension representing all of the material or biological dimensions of the human being. The second ball that both includes and transcends the first ball would represent the psychic or mental/emotional dimension. The third ball, the largest of the three, would represent the noetic or spiritual dimension. It would include all that is the somatic dimension and the psychic dimension and would transcend them both.

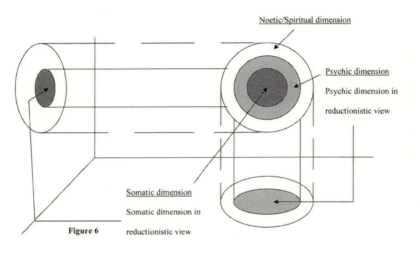

Figure 6

In this view, when a human being is looked at with eyes that only "see" the color of the somatic/biological dimension, the person is seen as only that size and color. The rest of the human being is "invisible" to someone unable to see what he or she is not looking for. The representation still has someone seen as a human being, but the interpretation of what a human being consists of is certainly "colored" by the vision of the one who is doing the looking. When one is looking with certain biological assumptions that determine the boundaries of the human being, the portions of the psychic and noetic dimensions that are inherently a part of the human being and together make the human being a living soul are at work in the somatic dimension, but they are not seen for what they truly are. They are only ancillary to the dimension that is actually under study due to the presuppositions of those who are doing the looking.

Physicians are one of the major categories of people who are trained to view the biological or somatic dimension. They often look for "cause and effect" relationships that can help them explain and treat biological illnesses. Physicians may very well give credence to the relative nature of the human psyche and even in some cases, to the human spirit in terms of desire, peace, and motivation, but all of these considerations are defined and seen in ways that bring about biological results. In some cases, physicians see only a small relationship with the psychic dimension and no relationship at all with the noetic or spiritual dimension. While only the highest form of reductionism would allow a physician to see a patient as strictly a biological cause and effect machine, a more universal form of reductionism is practiced by those who, while recognizing the interaction between the dimensions, would limit the dimension to no transcendence and see the entirety of the human being as contained in the somatic dimension.

Psychologists and psychiatrists are likewise susceptible to this more universal form of reductionism. While some, mostly psychiatrists, see the psyche in terms of a cause and effect machine and treat the patient accordingly, there are some who agree with many psychologists who see the human being as a much more involved combination of interrelated dimensions. Their view of the human being often sees the psychic dimension as the fundamental dimension in the human being. It includes the somatic but transcends it with conscious, subconscious, and unconscious activity. While this activity often, if not always, effects the somatic realities in human beings, it is still considered as something beyond the somatic dimension. Being a "higher" dimension, it includes somatic dimension but also transcends it.

Integrated Nature of Human Dimensional Ontology

Dr. Frankl, and, I believe, most Logotherapists and Logophilosophers see the noetic dimension as the uniquely human dimension, and, as such, the "highest" of the human dimensions. As such, it is the most inclusive of all of the dimensions. It includes the somatic dimension and the psychic dimension and transcends them both.

The reason why I particularly like the representation in Figure 6 is because it clearly portrays the way in which the dimensions are interdependent. They cannot function without one another and yet they are not equal. The noetic dimension, being inclusive and yet transcendent, becomes the largest storehouse for truly human resources with which a person can direct his or her life. It includes all of the resources of the somatic and the psychic dimensions and yet transcends them both offering in addition, resources that are purely noetic or spiritual.

While we have quickly examined the interrelatedness of the human dimensions, it is also imperative that we examine the dynamic nature of these same dimensions. These dimensions are both interrelated and dynamic. The ways in which they interact are what make human beings truly human. Figure 7 represents my understanding of the primary ways in which these human dimensions dynamically interact.

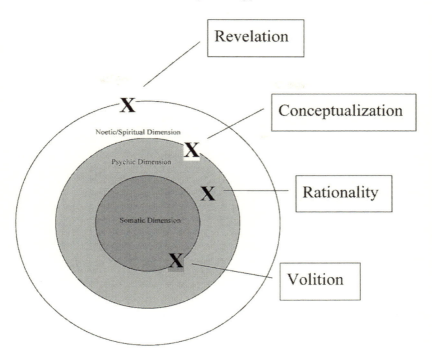

Figure 7

The somatic dimension is the smallest of the human dimensions. It is permeated with the psychic and the noetic dimensions (not separate from them) and must have a small measure of both at work within it in order to have life. Even reflex actions (or reactions) require some measure of life in order to function. The biological functioning of a human being (not dependent on any extraneous form of life support) requires a measure of thought and even of meaning in order to function. With no brain activity and no extraneous form of life support, the human body will cease to function. Even with a minimal level of brain activity, some measure of meaning or purpose is necessary for the human body to continue to function, even if the meaning or purpose is fundamental and minimal. The fundamental purpose can be as minimal as desiring to survive or satisfying a need such as hunger or thirst. Without any meaning or purpose, the human body will cease to function.

The somatic dimension seems to be very large, being composed of the "real" or material substances of the universe. However, as large as it truly is, it is still the smallest of the human dimensions. The psychic dimension includes the entire somatic dimension and transcends it.

The smallest thought is larger than the entirety of the somatic dimension. When we hear the word "universe," of what do we think? If we have been well educated, we will think of all of the material substances in existence including the space and vacuum in which they exist. (We will never see or experience all of these substances, thus we sense that in a specific context, this dimension is the largest.) It is, however, our ability to conceptualize "all the material substances in existence" that allows us firstly, to have a sense of what this means, and secondly, to manipulate the substances, change conditions, and "do" things. This is how we fly and how we travel in space and how we map the human genome. This is how we learn and how we operate in the realm of science.

Volition

The psychic dimension transcends the somatic dimension. The primary activity that relates these two dimensions is volition. Volition consists of decision and instruction. It is the activity of making a decision where more than one opportunity exists and then instructing the somatic dimension to bring that decision into the real or material world. It may be as simple as deciding what to say or what to write, in which case we bring the words, symbols, or actions into the material world through our voices, or by writing, or drawing, or motions of acting, or signs that have some meaning that is shared by others in the material world. Volition is an operation of the mind that expresses itself through the somatic dimension into the material world.

Volition or **will** is the cognitive process by which an individual decides on and commits to a particular course of action. It is defined as purposive striving, and is one of the primary human psychological functions (the others being **affection** [affect or feeling], **motivation** [goals and expectations] and **cognition** [thinking]). Volitional processes can be applied consciously, and they can be automized as habits over time. Most modern conceptions of volition address it as a process of action control that becomes automized (see e.g., Heckhausen and Kuhl; Gollwitzer; Corno and Kanfer).

Willpower is the colloquial, and volition the scientific, term for the same state of the will; viz., an "elective preference". When we have "made up our minds" (as we say) to a thing, i. e., have a settled state of choice respecting it, that state is called an immanent volition; when we put forth any particular act of choice, that act is called an immanant, or executive, or imperative, volition. When an immanent, or settled state of choice, is one which controls or governs a series of actions, we call that state a predominant volition; while we give the name of subordinate volitions to those particular acts of choice which carry into effect the object sought for by the governing or "predominant volition".

Within Gary Kielhofner's "Model of Human Occupation" volition is one of the three sub-systems that act on human behavior. Within this model volition considers a person's values, interests and beliefs about self-efficacy and personal capacity (Kielhofner, 2008, pp. 33-50).

Volition is the activity of the "freedom of the will" that Dr. Frankl states is one of the foundations of Logotherapy. While "freedom of the will" is essential to the exercise of Logotherapy, volition, by itself, is not inherently good. Neither is it inherently evil. It can be used for good or for evil purposes. It is the activity that is at the junction point of where the psychic activity transcends the somatic activity of the human being. The body does not "think" as the mind does. The body may react reflexively to certain stimuli, but it does not think. Some of the current discoveries in microbiology may tend to look as if the material of the human cell makes certain decisions, but the results are also understood as predetermined (if not completely understood) genetic reactions.

The human mind does think. Unless or until it is interfered with by disease or biological manipulation, the human mind is made to use volition. The fact that humans are able to make decisions is what gives credence to the idea that human beings are also responsible for their decisions. This "responsibility" is also central to Logotherapy. It is when humans act with some measure of responsibleness that they are truly human.

Rationalization

Volition is the activity that links the somatic dimension to the psychic dimension, which includes it (the somatic dimension) and also transcends it. Volition is not the only activity of the psychic dimension. Rationality is also part of the psychic dimension.

Rationality is the process of comparing and combining thoughts to form new thoughts. It is the process of "thought invention." It is a high form of thinking and it is a normal form of thinking for human beings.

The process of rationality would rightly be understood as rationalization, however, that term has been "hijacked" by negative connotations in the field of psychology. It has come to mean the process of constructing a logical justification for a decision that was originally arrived at through a different mental process. It insinuates that logic dictates an activity that a human being feels then needs to justify by substituting a reason other than the most fundamental one that was used in the process of decision-making. An example would be when a person buys a car because they like the style and the power of the engine, but they say that they bought the car because of its good gas mileage in order to make the decision more acceptable to himself or herself or to others. Rationalization is more than making acceptable excuses to oneself! In truth, doing so, represents the activity of a process that is normal for the mind.

That process is the ability to take two or more thoughts and compare, contrast, and combine them in such a way that new thoughts are formed as a result of the process. This is the normal way of thinking for human beings. The ability to "rationalize" in this way is what gives human beings the ability to function in situations where relationships with other people or things are the norm. Communication requires this process so we can send the meaning out into the real world in symbols or sounds that can be related to by other human beings who in turn use the process of rationalization to "interpret" or seek the meaning from those same symbols or sounds. This is the "thinking" process of the human mind.

Conceptualization

Conceptualization is the activity that relates the psychic dimension and the noetic or spiritual dimension. Conceptualization is the activity of turning meaning into ideas and ideas into thoughts. Forming a conceptualization is the first stage of knowledge representation. It takes meaning that is ontologically present but not rationally understood and moves it into the psychic dimension where it can begin to be "rationalized" and processed through the activity of thinking. Concepts are those meaning bearers that allow us to form thoughts that become the agents of meaning.

The noetic or spiritual dimension of a human being includes all that is somatic and all that is psychic and transcends it so that there is an area of human ontology that is solely noetic or spiritual. It is in this dimension that human beings interact most purely, but not most completely, with meaning.

The most complete interaction that human beings have with meaning is in the somatic dimension where all of the human dimensions are involved with the interaction. In the somatic dimension there are elements of all of the human dimensions at work. The relationship of our thoughts, words, and deeds, to the ontological reality of meaning is influenced by the way in which we are able to incorporate the psychic and noetic dimensions in the somatic expressions of life. The more we can incorporate the psychic and noetic dimensions and their interrelated activities of conceptualization, rationalization, and volition, within the somatic expressions of our living, the more human we will be. By doing so we will be wiser, deeper, and better able to relate to all of life in a way that expresses the true dimension of the meanings that are present in life. It is by doing so that we better understand and live our purpose in life, which is another of the foundations of Logotherapy.

Revelation

The activity that relates human beings to the ontological reality in which they exist is the activity of revelation. In a religious sense, revelation is used to denote a divine communication with God whereby divine knowledge is imparted and human knowledge is the result. In a phenomenological and ontological sense, revelation is our relationship to that which exists beyond our being and yet becomes part of our being. In the case of Logotherapy and

Logophilosophy, the ontological reality in which we exist is the reality of meaning. Meaning exists all around us and is, therefore, discoverable as it is revealed to us. In a real sense, meaning includes all that is human (dimensionally speaking) and transcends it as well.

The existence of meaning as that which we live in and yet transcends us is what allows us to discover meaning. While meaning can, and most often is, discovered through our somatic relationships with the expressions of meaning in the world around us, it can also be discovered through the activity or process of revelation. Who has not felt the assurance of "knowing something" that he or she could not put into words or actions? This is the fundamental aspect of faith and is essential to the activity of having faith in someone or something. Who can explain the depth of love that one can discover which can be explained in words or actions, but not fully or completely so? Who can fully understand the roots of passion that would lead a person to live for another or for a cause other than rudimentary self-interest?

All of these examples, and many more, express the ontological reality of meaning that permeates and yet transcends the entirety of the human dimensions. This view of human ontology allows for the true "largeness" of the noetic or spiritual dimension while preserving the important, even essential notions of Logotherapy and Logophilosopy with one noted exception. How do we portray wholeness and the true integration of this ontology throughout human consciousness?

Wholeness and the Nature of Human Dimensional Ontology

First let us focus on the issue of integration of the dimensions throughout the spectrum of human consciousness. We will see why and how the human dimensions are integrated and why that integration is often misunderstood. Then we will focus on why the noetic dimension is the storehouse of human healing resources. This will give us a better understanding of the reason for Logotherapy as well as the benefits it offers to the healing sciences.

Integration

Dr. Frankl, in contrast to Dr. Freud, believed that "any human phenomenon, whether belonging to the personal axis or to the somatic-psychic layers, may occur on any level, the unconscious, preconscious or conscious" (Frankl, 1975, p. 30). Freud saw that the unconscious was always and only instinctual in nature and was, more than anything else, a "reservoir of repressed instinctuality." According to Dr. Frankl,

> It might be said that psychoanalysis has id-ified, and de-selv-ified, human existence. Insofar as Freud degraded the self to a mere epiphenomenon, he betrayed the self and delivered it to the id; at the same time, he denigrated the unconscious, in that he saw in it only the instinctual and overlooked the spiritual (Frankl, 1975, p. 27).

The key to the integration of the human dimensions with human consciousness is found in the necessity of transcendence. For Dr. Frankl, existence had an inescapable quality of self-transcendence. While some would see a human as a closed system of cause and effect, others could see a human as open to the world. Dr. Frankl says:

> That the self-transcendent quality of existence, the openness of being human, is touched by one cross section and missed by another is understandable. Closedness and openness have become compatible. And I think that the same holds true of freedom and determinism. There is determinism in the psychological dimension, and freedom in the noological dimension, which is the human dimension, the dimension of human phenomena. As to the body-

mind problem, we wound up with the phrase "unity in spite of diversity." As to the problem of free choice, we are winding up with the phrase "freedom in spite of determinism." It parallels the phrase once coined by Nicolai Hartmann, "autonomy in spite of dependency."

As a human phenomenon, however, freedom is all too human. Human freedom is finite freedom. Man is not free from conditions. But he is free to take a stand in regard to them. The conditions do not completely condition him. Within limits it is up to him whether or not he succumbs and surrenders to the conditions (Frankl, 1978, p. 47).

But we must not neglect the fact that being human is always individualized being. As such, it is always centered around a core, and this core is the person, who, in the words of Max Scheler, is not only the agent but also the "center" of spiritual activity.

Being centered around the existential, personal, spiritual core, human being is not only individualized but also integrated.

Wholeness in this context means the integration of somatic, psychic and spiritual aspects. It is not possible to stress enough that it is only this three-fold wholeness which makes man complete. In no way are we justified in speaking of man in terms of only a "somatic-psychic whole" (Frankl, 1975, p. 28).

While the dividing line between the unconscious and the conscious is "fluid" and crossed often from both directions, i.e. making the unconscious conscious and making the conscious "repressed" or unconscious, the dividing line between the spiritual and the instinctual is resolutely sharp and must remain that way. The instinctual flows from the somatic level to the psychic dimension.

Instinct is defined in various ways. For most psychologists and sociologists, instinct is defined as any behavior that is repeated. In addition it is seen as an inherent disposition toward a particular behavior. Instincts are considered as fixed patterns of action. Such things as reproduction, feeding, courtship, the building of nests, and the biological predisposition of a colt to learn to stand, walk and run with the herd are all examples of instinctual behavior in animals.

The scientific definition of instinct has had a long and varied use. From the earliest psychological laboratory of Wilhelm Wundt in the late nineteenth century, through the 1960's conference on instinct led by Frank Beach, to the most current psychology textbooks of the twenty-first century, the use and acceptance of the term has changed. In fact the only mention of the word "instinct" in the top twelve best selling psychology textbooks in the year 2000 was in relation to Freud's reference to the "id" instincts.

Any repeated behavior can be called "instinctual." As can any behavior for which there is a strong innate component. However, to distinguish behavior beyond the control of the organism from behavior that has a repetitive component we can turn to the book "Instinct"(1961) stemming from the 1960 conference. A number of criteria were established which distinguishes instinctual from other kinds of behavior. To be considered instinctual a behavior must a) be automatic, b) be irresistible, c) occur at some point in development, d) be triggered by some event in the environment, e) occur in every member of the species, f) be unmodifiable, and g) govern behavior for which the organism needs no training (although the organism may profit from experience and to that degree the behavior is modifiable). The absence of one or more of these criteria indicates that the behavior is not fully instinctual. Instincts do exist in insects and animals as can be seen in behaviors that can not be changed by learning. Psychologists recognize that humans do have biological predispositions or behaviors that are easy to learn due to biological wiring, for example walking and talking. If these criteria are used in a rigorous scientific manner, application of the term "instinct" cannot be used in reference to human behavior. When terms, such as mothering, territoriality, eating, mating, and so on, are used to denote human behavior they are seen to not meet the criteria listed above. In comparison to animal behavior such as hibernation, migration, nest building, mating and so on that are clearly instinctual, no human behavior meets the necessary criteria. And even in regard to animals, in many cases if the correct learning is stopped from occurring these instinctual behaviors disappear, suggesting that they are potent, but limited, biological predispostions. In the final analysis, under this definition, there are no human instincts (Beach, 2008).

If, indeed, instinct in humans can be agreed to mean motivation toward specific actions in response to particular stimuli, then we can better understand the meaning of instincts as the term relates to human beings and Logotherapy. For Dr. Frankl, the true importance of the difference between instinctual and spiritual is found in the following:

Since human existence is spiritual existence, we now see that the distinction between conscious and unconscious becomes unimportant compared with another distinction: The real criterion of authentically human existence only derives from discerning whether a given phenomenon is spiritual or instinctual – whereas it is relatively irrelevant whether it is conscious or unconscious. This is due to the fact that – in contrast to the psychoanalytic concept – being human is not being driven but "deciding what one is going to be," to quote Jaspers (*entscheidendes Sein*), or to quote Heidegger: *Dasein.* I would say that being human is being responsible – existentially responsible, responsible for one's own existence.

Existence thus may well be authentic even when it is unconscious; on the other hand, man only exists authentically when he is not driven but, rather, responsible. Authentic existence is present where a self is deciding for himself, but not where an id is driving him (Frankl, 1975, pp. 26-27).

In order to visualize this appropriately, I would suggest that we need to add to Dr. Frankl's visualizations in the following way. In Figure 8 one can see the deliniation of the conscious, preconscious, and unconscious in the way that they are described by Dr. Frankl. That which is unconscious can become preconscious or conscious by coming primarily from the somatic dimension (realized as instincts) or from the spiritual dimension as the unconscious spirit. Focusing on the one (realized instincts) will make us less than fully human while the only way to be authentically human, according to the tenets of Logotherapy, is to focus on those traits that accompany the human spirit which includes and transcends the other (lower or less inclusive) dimensions of the human being.

Dr. Frankl redefines "depth psychology" in Logotherapeutic terms. Depth psychology is referred to as any psychology that operates with the assumption of an unconscious mind. The inclusion of the noetic dimension and the idea of unconscious spirit causes Dr. Frankl to think in terms of "height psychology" by taking the idea of the unconscious into all of the human dimensions. He states that the unconscious, preconscious and conscious are at work in all of the human dimensions. While instincts (unconscious and preconscious somatic needs) drive us for their fulfillment, the will to meaning that flows from the noetic unconscious and preconscious *draw* us toward fulfillment through meaning and purpose in life.

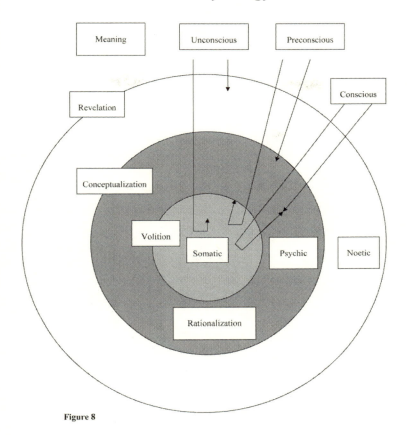

Figure 8

In Figure 8 we can see the flow of unconscious to preconscious to conscious coming from both the somatic/psychic dimensions and from the noetic or spiritual dimension. This figure allows one to visualize the relationship of the human dimensions with the human consciousness as well as see the interaction between the human dimensions. Since each of the human dimensions includes the dimension(s) lower than itself but transcends it (them), we can see how all of the levels of consciousness are at work in all of the dimensions. We can also see that there is a noetic unconscious that draws the human being toward the fulfillment of those aspects that are inherent in the noetic dimension's existence; i.e., meaning, the will to meaning, and purpose in life. These are the foundational tennets of Logotherapy. This allows us to see a holistic view of the integration of the human dimensions and better understand how Dr. Frankl's wholeness model of integration relates to the interaction between and within the human dimensions.

Storehouse of Healing Resources

The noetic dimension is the storehouse of human healing resources. Within it lies the strength of meaning that is yet to be realized and pulls the human being toward its own fulfillment. Who can understand the full meaning of love or creativity or faith that takes a stand in the face of unavoidable suffering? These meanings find their expression in the life of the human being by focusing outwardly into the relationships that a human being has with the world of things and people that surround him or her.

> The noetic dimension contains the essence of life and the noetic unconscious contains the voice of meaning. As pointed out, the noetic dimension is like the medicine chest of logotherapy containing the resources of the human spirit: The noetic unconscious might be understood as the reservoir of these resources. This is the place within our humanness where we hear the call to meaning in the circumstances and events of our lives (Graber, 2000, p. 78).

The most powerful resources for maximizing our human potential are found in the noetic dimension. Beginning with the noetic unconscious, we find a great number of meanings that draw us toward our human fulfillment. Our will to meaning, itself, is found there. Love, creativity, and faith are found there. These meanings move from an unconscious state to a preconscious state to conscious thoughts and ideas. As such, they motivate specifically human actions. These actions are human when they are a result of the self deciding for itself to transcend itself.

The areas of meaning discovery are most pertinent to this study. They include love, creativity, and attitude toward suffering. These areas are key to Logotherapy and Logophilosophy. They will be studied in depth in the next chapter.

CHAPTER IV
FRANKLIAN METHODS OF MEANING DISCOVERY

One of the key areas of Logotherapy and Logophilosophy is the area of meaning discovery. In his earliest work, *Man's Search for Meaning*, Dr. Frankl makes it clear that even though the meaning of life always changes, it never ceases to exist. According to Logotherapy there are three different ways that meaning can be discovered. These ways are:
1) by creating something or by doing a deed,
2) by experiencing something or encountering someone with loving someone or something being the highest form of encounter, and
3) by the attitude we take toward unavoidable suffering (Frankl, 1959, p. 133).

For Dr. Frankl, discovering meaning is a spiritual act with eternal consequences. He expresses that the boundary of eternity is found in the present. It is in the present moment that humans choose what they want to admit into the eternity of the past. He believes in the activism of the future and the optimism of the past. Dr. Frankl sees the demand quality of life as the reality of our human responsibleness as life in the present presents us with the opportunity to choose what we will admit into our eternal record.

> Everything is written into the eternal record – our whole life, all our creations and actions, encounters and experiences, all our loving and suffering. All this is contained, and remains, in the eternal record. The world is not, as the great existential philosopher Karl

Jaspers intimated, a manuscript written in a code we have to decipher: no, the world is rather a record that we must dictate.

This record is of a dramatic nature, for day by day life is asking us questions, we are interrogated by life, and we have to answer. *Life*, I would say, *is a life-long question-and-answer period.* As to the answers, I do not weary of saying that we can only answer to life by answering *for* our lives.

The eternal record cannot be lost – that is a comfort and a hope. But neither can it be corrected – and that is a warning and a reminder. It reminds us that, as nothing can be removed from the past, all the more it is up to us to rescue our chosen possibilities into the past. It now turns out that logotherapy presents not only an "optimism of the past" (in contrast to existentialism's "pessimism of the present") but also an "activism of the future" (in contrast to quietism's "fatalism of eternity"). For if everything is stored in the past forever, it is important to decide in the present what we wish to eternalize by making it part of the past. This is the secret of creativity: that we are moving something from the nothingness of the future into the "being past" (Frankl, 1978, pp. 110-111).

Creative Activity

Creative activity is the best known of the three ways to discover meaning. It is the process of bringing something into being that did not exist in a substantial way previous to the creative activity. It is the process of taking an idea or a concept and bringing it into the somatic (material) reality of the world in which we live and move and have our being. Or it can be the activity of taking something (or some things) that exist and putting them together in such a way that something new is created that did not exist previously. Since creative activity involves the use of our talents and abilities, it is an activity that is interactive and becomes meaningful for us.

Creative activity also involves learning and growing as a human being. Part of the meaning of creative activity is found in the ways in which it helps us to learn about ourselves and our talents as well as the world around us. Using words to create a story a poem or a paper helps us learn more about the subject that is related to the world through the words as well as learning more about ourselves and our thinking. It can even help us better understand our theology, philosophy, and world view (weltanschauung). Artists use the materials of their mediums to bring ideas, feelings, and meanings into a concrete form; a painting, a sculpture, pottery, beadwork, or a number of other items. Most of the artists I know (myself included) learn more about themselves as well as their medium of expression with each work of art that is created.

The discovery of meaning through creative activity is an invitation of sorts from the world around us to enter into life and become fully engaged in it. It is life asking us to use our talents to add to life's value, for that is exactly what a meaningful existence does. It adds the value of meaning to existence.

By engaging life through the discovery of meaning in creative activity, we are also invited to enjoy the fullness of a meaningful life. Enjoying the work that has been created allows for more meaning to be discovered through the encounters we have with the objects that have been created. It is a gift of meaning that keeps on giving meaning.

Another form of creative activity is the accomplishment of a task. The doing of a deed is a type of creativity. Something that was an idea becomes a reality in the somatic dimension of the real world through our speaking or through our doing. Doing a deed creates a new relationship with the world around us. Cleaning a room, writing in a journal, calling a friend, helping a neighbor – all of these things and countless more – help us to understand that turning an idea into an action that accomplishes something is a way to discover meaning.

Task oriented people seem to find an additional measure of meaning in the accomplishment of tasks. The setting of a goal, the pursuit of that goal, and the accomplishment of that goal, even in part, can provide a number of tasks that can be accomplished adding to the meaning of fulfillment in life. The doing of deeds, while not as concrete as other forms of creativity, creates the opportunity for meaningful memories to be stored and revisited. The remembering of deeds done, goals met, tasks accomplished also brings the very real feeling of meaning back again and again through our memories. This reflective enjoyment is another sense of fulfillment that can come through discovering meaning through creative activity and the doing of a deed.

Experiences

Another way to discover meaning is through our experiences. This is particularly the case when our experiences include the encountering of other people or other significant things. This type of meaning discovery comes at the behest of our choosing to recognize it. It is not the result of an accomplishment as is meaning discovered through creativity. It is the meaning that surrounds us in life and simply needs to be recognized. It is the meaning that is discovered in relationships.

Experiential meaning can be discovered as we choose how we will relate to the people and things around us. The highest and most human choice we can make is to love someone or something. Truly loving someone or something is an act that demands transcendence. Love requires the extension of our being through thoughts, words and deeds that are aimed at the betterment of life for the person or thing that we love. Only a perverted form of selfishness can pass as "love" when our own benefit is sought at the expense of others. Love is the highest form of experiential meaning discovery.

While we do not do anything to accomplish meaning discovered by experience, we do make decisions that affect our relationships. Love is a decsion that affects our relationships. When we decide to love something or someone, we are making a truly human decision. When we choose to love somone we are deciding to "get outside of" ourselves and focus on the betterment and true fulfillment of another person. When we choose to love something of true importance, we are choosing to relate to that "thing" in a way that helps to bring about its fulfillment in existence.

Genuinely loving someone is a truly selfless act. It is not done in order to get something in return for the love that is given. It is chosen as a relationship that helps to bring about the betterment or fulfillment of the person who is the object of the love. We need not be present with the person or people we choose to love in order to love them. A person can choose to love the orphaned children of Africa without ever seeing them or being present with them and can still live out that love in ways that work for the true betterment and fulfillment of those children.

Love, as an experiencial choice, is not limited to people. We can choose to love things in ways that give true meaning discovery. A person may choose to love golf in a truly meaningful way. In doing so, the person will work for the betterment of the game of golf and truly appreciate the enjoyment and benefits that come from participating in the game of golf. They may choose to give of themselves in meaningful ways to help others learn and enjoy the benefits of the game as well. As an experiencial choice, love is not limited to people.

Even though love is the highest form of human choice for experiencial meaning discovery, it is by no means the only form. When we make the choice to be open to the experiences of life around us and to fully participate in life, we can discover meaning in an enormous variety of experiences. The Native

Americans viewed life in this world as the opportunity to live in harmony with all that surrounded them. A gentle breeze, a good hunt, a good day of tending peach trees, all of these things and much more could offer opportunities to find meaning in the experiences of life. Finding meaning in the experiences of life was part of the nature of living that made the experience of life sacred rather than mundane. Living in harmony with one's surroundings was considered the most meaningful of all ways to live. It was (and is) the good path.

Attitudes

This method of meaning discovery is what Logotherapy is most noted for helping to recognize. It is the attitude taken toward unavoidable suffering that provides the opportunity for genuine meaning discovery. When one finds oneself in the midst of the inescapable suffering of life, the choice remains ours to decide how we will face the suffering. Through four Nazi concentration camps, Dr. Frankl witnessed and practiced the type of decision-making that led to the discovery of meaning in the worst of circumstances. He experienced the difference that making the right decision can make. He saw many people give in to what they considered their fate and die more quickly as a result. Those who took a stand in the face of unavoidable suffering and even inescapable death were able to find meaning in their lives that continued until the end of their lives. Dr. Frankl, himself, came to a time where he was so depressed that he was close to falling into the abyss of a meaningless death due to his circumstances when a friend in the camp had a serious conversation with him and brought him face to face with the "demand quality of life" and his own opportunity to find meaning in the midst of it. This point of turn-around was important to Dr. Frankl and to the development of Logotherapy.

Many are the examples of people who face the tragic news of a chronic or even deadly illness with a decision to make the most of the life that they have to live. Dr. Robert Barnes, when struck with a debilitating paralysis, made the choice to live his life to the fullest, helping as many people as he could every day. As a counselor and an educator, he has influenced the lives of hundreds of thousands of people through his work and research on five continents and as the President of the Viktor Frankl Institute of Logotherapy. His demeaner and his obvious commitment to discovering meaning in the midst of suffering have led him to be honored on many occasions and in many places as one who lives out the truth of Logotherapy.

In his book, *The Doctor and the Soul*, Dr. Frankl explains that suffering is a natural part of the human condition. What he labels "the tragic triad" of guilt, pain, and death can make people despondent. The "neurotic triad" of aggression, depression, and addiction puts people in despair while the "existential vacuum" can cause doubt and confusion by blocking the noetic dimension of human existence.

Dr. Lukas, in her wonderful book, *Meaning in Suffering*, describes many such incidents. She says,

> On the assumption that unavoidable suffering can be borne if a meaning can be seen in it, logotherapy tries to bring the suffering into connection with a meaning the patient can accept. This is not always easy.
> Case No. 14; A 40 year-old man came to see me and asked if I could find a good home for his infant, "if need be." When I inquired what he meant by "if need be," he broke down, sobbing. He told me that his wife had inoperable cancer, and the physicians had expected her to die before the child was born. As by a miracle the baby was born healthy.
> I promised the man to look out for a good home, and he asked if I would tell this to his wife, too, because she too worried about the child's future. I asked them

to meet me the next day. This case illustrates how insignificant the question of competency becomes in the face of the unavoidable. Psychologists do not find homes for infants – but I was not asked as a psychologist. I was challenged as a human being.

The next day I asked them to tell me about their life together. They were married six years, had always been close, more so since the wife's illness. The child was an unexpected gift that had stirred their emotions deeply, especially since it turned out so unexpectedly well.

When they finished, there was a pause. Then I told them something like this: "Mr. and Mrs. X, I congratulate you both heartily. You have shown in your short shared life so much mutual love and courage as very few couples, even after 30 or 40 years of marriage experience. Hundreds of married couples come to our counseling center, and what I hear are trivial disputes, selfishness, and mutual distrust. Only rarely will two people relate so happily as you have. This is something to be proud of, because what matters is not how long two people live together but how intensely they fill their lives with mutual respect and love. If I add the hours of harmony in many of the marriages where both partners have the good fortune to live a long life, the total hours of harmony would hardly approach the six years you were able to live happily together. No one can take away those past years and you deserve to be congratulated.

The husband's eyes were moist, and the wife reached out for my hand. "I am not unhappy about the fate that will separate us soon," she said, "I'm worried about my husband. I am afraid he may lose his hold, when he is alone." "But, Mrs. X," I relplied. "You do leave him a hold on life, there is hardly a stronger kind – a task for which he is responsible: the child of your love. No one who is aware of a task which he knows he has to fulfill, will lose his grip, he will even find strength to help others. Your husband will remain strong, even when you are no longer with him, strong enough to support the child and to bring it up well." Here the husband jumped to his feet, knelt before his wife and solemnly promised to find the strength to bring up the child as long as it needed his care. They left our counseling center serenely and confidently, though no circumstances had changed.

What was helpful in this logotherapeutic discourse was not "comfort" – there can hardly be comfort for a person facing death. Here the important thing was finding some meaning connected with the two questions weighing on them. Why did their happy togetherness have to end so suddenly, and what would happen after the wife's death? If a short married life had brought more happy hours than many a long marriage, then the number of hours and years is less important than content. The six happy years retain their meaning even when abruptly ended. The woman knows she has left the child to her husband, a task and a support to help him over his sorrow: the birth of the child before her death is a powerful legacy of their mutual love, transcending death. The tragedy of the inevitable is softened by the awareness of a fulfilled life (Lukas, 1986, pp. 65-66).

Finding meaning in unavoidable suffering is not an easy task, but it is most certainly a possible task. It is, in fact, the work of the human soul that makes the human being most authentically human. The exercise of this human facility makes it possible to find meaning in every situation in life.

From the beginning of Logotherapy through to its current status, the views of Dr. Frankl on meaning discovery have been a significant touchstone of Logotherapy. These three areas or forms of meaning discovery are a connecting link to the relationship between Logotherapy and Christianity. The presence of meaning, itself, is the connecting constant of this relationship. The importance of meaning discovery 1) by creating something or by doing a deed, 2) by experiencing something or encountering someone with loving someone or something being the highest form of encounter, and 3) by the attitude we take toward unavoidable suffering (Frankl, 1959, p. 133) will become abundantly clear as we examine the relationship between Franklian thought and Christian spiritual formation.

CHAPTER V
"THE THREE WAYS" OF CHRISTIAN SPIRITUAL FORMATION

The classical understanding of Christian spiritual formation is described in a context known as "the three ways." The one person who did the most to bring the literature together concerning this context is Evelyn Underhill. Her first important book entitled *Mysticism* is the classic text for launching forward or backward in a study of the three ways. Her work has been expanded by many writers since the 1911 publishing of the book, but arguably the best book which expands and further explains the context and the journey of the three ways is the book *Spiritual Passages* by Benedict Groeschel.

Evelyn Underhill was born in 1875, and grew up as the child of a lawyer in Wolverhampton. Her education was begun at home as a private education. She later finished at a private school in Folkestone. She then went to King's College for Women in London. She was married in 1907 and converted from agnosticism to Christianity that same year in spite of the objections of her husband. She was most attracted to Roman Catholicism. Later in her life, in 1921, she became an Anglican.

From the time of her conversion her life was filled with religious work. She was quite fond of St. Teresa's saying that "to give Our Lord a perfect service Martha and Mary must combine." She wrote in the mornings and gave her afternoons to visiting the poor and working as a spiritual director. As she became older more and more of her time was devoted to spiritual direction. She led retreats and wrote a great deal about philosophy and religion. She lived at the time of the birthing and growth of psychology and was an ardent student. She considered psychology on a par with philosophy and religion when it came to understanding the call of God upon the life of a person to move into wholeness.

Evelyn Underhill establishes the basis for a thorough examination of mysticism as well as its acceptance as a scientific way to approach the reality of the human longing for the absolute. She writes:

> . . . it now seems to me that a critical realism, which found room for the duality of our full human experience – the Eternal and the Successive, supernatural and natural reality – would provide a better philosophic background to the experience of the mystics than the vitalism which appeared, twenty years ago, to offer so promising a way of escape from scientific determinism. Determinism – more and more abandoned by its old friends the physicists – is no longer the chief enemy to such a spiritual interpretation of life as is required by the experience of the mystics. It is rather a naturalistic monism, a shallow doctrine of immanence unbalanced by any adequate sense of transcendence, which now threatens to re-model theology in a sense which leaves no room for the noblest and purest reaches of the spiritual life (Underhill, 1911, p. xiv).

Sadly, this argument is cogent in our time, nearly one hundred years later. One cannot help but see the parallel concerns between Underhill in Christian spirituality and Frankl in psychology. From the beginning they each identified the sad reality of their time which was scientific determinism and reductionism. They each also stood mightily for the acknowledgement of the "whole" person in the midst of a time that wanted to discount the very foundations of their understandings of human wholeness.

For Underhill, it was necessary to fight for the recovery of the supernatural.

The recovery of the concept of the Supernatural – a word which no respectable theologian of the last generation cared to use – is closely linked with the great name of Friedrich von Hugel. His persistent opposition to all merely monistic, pantheist and immanental philosophies of religion, and his insistence on the need of a "two-step diagram" of the Realtiy accessible to man, though little heeded in his life-time, are now bearing fruit. This re-instatement of the Transcendent, the "Wholly Other," as *the* religious fact, is perhaps the most fundamental of the philosophic changes which have directly affected the study of mysticism (Underhill, 1911, p. xv).

At the beginning of the Christian period there are three sources of the mystical tradition. They are Greek, Oriental, and Christian. The Christian tradition began as the primitive Apostolic doctrine or thought. A chronology of the development of mysticism as the definition of what has now become Christian spiritual formation or the formation of souls would include St. Paul, Clement of Alexandria, Origen, and, even though he was not a Christian, but a philosopher, Plotinus. Even though Plotinus' mysticism does not come from the Christian faith, he influences following generations of Christians with his Platonic philosophy. His most favorite student, Porphyry, developed a Neoplatonism that became a confused, semi-religious philosophy. It took the development of mysticism in a different direction from the direction that developed through the Christian community.

Even though it was indirect, the influence of Plotinus on the early Christian mystics was rather large. St. Augustine and Dionysius the Areopagite were part of that group that was greatly influenced. The Egyptian Fathers of the desert represent another strain of Christian mysticism that is equally important. St. Marcarius of Egypt was a student of St. Anthony and St. Basil. His teachings reached the west through John Cassian. At the beginning of the middle ages there were two distinct strains of mystical thought in the Christian community. These strains were the Benedictine and the Neoplatonic.

Through the middle ages these two strains were further developed. Christians such as John Scotus Erigena, St. Anselm, St. Bernard of Clairvaux, Joachim of Flora, Richard of St. Victor, and Hugh all have a part in the development of mysticism in the early part of the middle ages. As the middle ages progressed, the torch was carried by St. Francis of Assisi, John of Parma, and the "doctors" of the church such as St. Bonaventura and St. Thomas Aquinas.

Master Eckhart became a true leader in the movement to further the relationship of mystical insight and intense intellectual (German) thought. He was followed by those he greatly influenced, John Tauler, St. Teresa, and St. John of the Cross. Julian of Norwich is the last great English mystic of the middle ages though she was proceeded by two other great women mystics, St. Bridget of Sweden and St. Catherine of Siena.

The sixteenth and seventeenth centuries saw the movement of mysticism flow through Italy and begin in new strains of Christian experience. St. Ignatius of Loyola and St. John of the Cross were great influences in the development of mysticism. Jacob Boehme and George Fox represent two distinct strains of mysticism that flourished outside of the church of Rome. Jacob Boehme's thought spread far and wide as a symbolic, constructive, activistic understanding that used the language of regeneration. George Fox founded the Quaker movement and represents another outbreak of true mysticism. Even though his movement spurned the organized church, his thought and practice had much in common with the Quietist movement and the Catholic contemplatives of that time.

There was a large movement of mysticism in England outside of the church among the intellectual community in the seventeenth century. Within the Catholic church, the movement found its greatest expression in France.

The Catholic mysticism of this period is best seen in France, where the intellectual and social expansion of the Grande Siecle had also its spiritual side. Over against the brilliant worldly life of seventeenth century Paris and the slackness and even corruption of much organized religion, there sprang up something like a cult of the inner life. This mystical renaissance seems to have originated in the work of an English Capuchin friar, William Fitch, in religion Benedict Canfield, who settled in Paris in old age and there became a centre of spiritual influence (Underhill, 1911, p. 470).

Students of Benedict Canfield included Madame Acarie and Pierre de Berulle. They were responsible for spreading his teachings on contemplation to most of the great religious personalities of that time. Madame Acarie and her three daughters became Carmelite nuns. St. Francois de Sales was a youth member of Madame Acarie's circle. Outside of this circle, Brother Lawrence, a Carmelite friar, expressed the passive form of French mysticism.

The seventeenth century saw the rise and, at its end, the fall of the Quietist movement. Some elements of the movement were also housed in the German mystic and religious leader, Jacob Boehme. His student, John Gichtel, wrote much about Boehme's teachings in Germany. In England, Boehme's teachings influence the growth of Dionysius Andreas Freher who influenced William Law. Law was converted by reading Boehme's works.

The nineteenth and twentieth centuries saw a steep decline in mysticism. The rise of scholastic science and the growth of a secular, consumer oriented culture both gave rise to a secular science that displaced the mystery in mysticism. With Evelyn Underhill, mysticism became an object of study as much as a religious practice. She and the Catholic monk, Benedict

Groeschel, have done as much as anyone to influence the general public concerning the nature and practice of mysticism and its role in Christian spiritual formation. Other obvious influences would include Mother Teresa, Adrian Van Kaam, and Susan Muto.

A revival of sorts in the interest and practice of mysticism has grown from the Charismatic movement of the latter half of the twentieth century. As the popular segment of the movement made its way through the denominational churches and spawned non-denominational influence, the deeper study and longing for meaningful Christian spiritual growth that was not centered on a certain cultural context began to show itself in a genuine interest in Christian spiritual formation. This renewal of interest and practice has found Evelyn Underhill and Benedict Groeschel to be two of its most influencial advocates.

The three ways of Christian spiritual formation emerged from years of the practice of mysticism as the path to spiritual maturity. The form has coalesced over the years into a movement from The Purgative Way, to The Illuminative Way, to The Unitive Way. The purpose of this understanding of spiritual growth and maturity is for one to experience "Union with God" in a thoroughly Biblical context. This experience is the reason for Christian spiritual formation and the object of Christian spiritual maturity.

The Purgative Way

The entrance into the purgative way is marked by the acceptance of the Christian gospel: i.e., the acceptance of Jesus Christ as the Messiah of God. The acceptance of this belief is defined as the Christian conversion experience. The conversion is from one who does not believe to one who does believe. For some this transformation is accompanied by great emotional experiences. For others it is a simple matter of intellectual assent with the resulting life changes that rationally follow such a belief. For all Christians this belief begins a process of transformation that is often referred to as "being molded in the image of Christ." It is the process of Christian spiritual formation.

First Phase

The first phase of the way of purgation is the phase of moral integration. It is the phase of getting out of one's life those things that separate one from God and bringing into one's life those things that help one be molded in the image of Christ. It is a time of breaking old habits and healing old wounds. It is a time of moving toward the experience of freedom and recognizing the peace of the presence of God. It is the phase of a new beginning in Christ. Benedict Groeschel puts it this way:

> The new convert or the Christian recently aware of the life of the Spirit is drawn inexorably to change, growth, and a complexity of seemingly contradictory behaviors: the healing of old wounds and inflicting of new ones; growth in the Spirit and a decline in egotism; being filled with the strength of God and at the same time becoming utterly helpless. The precious gifts of life and time are not less important, but take on a transcendent importance (Groeschel, 1984, p. 103).

The moral integration phase is an intentional phase of purging the Christian's life from sin and its destructive power. The Sermon on the Mount is the foundation from which Christian moral integration takes place. It is a time of work and is seen by most spiritual directors as the most important and the most discouraging phase of spiritual development. On the other hand, it is also the time when the true peace of God and freedom from sin are first experienced in a genuine and lasting way. For that reason, it is also a time of the recognition of new power to discover meaning and to change.

While the focus of this first phase in the "way of purgation" is on moral integration, the experience of the one who is sincerely committed to this quest for union with God is initially one of temptation. Old habits are hard to break and one is reluctant to let go of them and the comfort that they bring. When one recognizes that one needs to rid one's lifes of a sin such as stealing, one will only notice the power of that sin when one is tempted to perform it. It is when one has the opportunity to defeat sin in one's life that one fully recognizes the power of temptation.

The spiritual Christian faces the beginning of the three ways by asking the question, "Do I live by the moral teachings of Christ?" This question becomes permanently important to the person who seeks to be molded in the image of Christ. Such a person never "arrives" at a state of being where this question is unimportant. It will always be the question of moral integration.

This question becomes even more important to us in this time of moral relativism. We live in a time where the very tools of Christian spiritual formation are being used to separate religious experience from holiness of life and "right living."

> The tendency to separate religious experience from rectitude of life represents an old and dangerous tradition of gnosticism at its worst – a tradition which, by the way, is contradicted by the lives and teachings of the saints (Groeschel, 1984, p. 104).

Growth through this or any phase of the three ways requires constant effort on the part of the person seeking union with God. Facing one's sins, receiving forgiveness, and overcoming the power of temptation are the hallmarks of this phase of spiritual development in the three ways. No one makes it through the first phase of the way of purgation without giving a full recognition to sin. Seeing what is in our lives that does not "look like Christ" is the first step toward purging our lives of that which does not "look like Christ." What one who is seriously on the path toward union with God discovers is the transforming power of the Holy Spirit of God at work in the life of the believer. The power of God to "break the power of cancelled sin" and to "set the prisoner free" is made evident in this first phase of the purgative way. It is this glorious freedom and the accompanying peace of the soul that invites, urges and draws one on toward the full meaning of God's redemption.

Second Phase
The second phase of the purgative way is the development of a mature faith. The focus is on a genuine trust of God. Faith and trust become the two central factors of the development of a life of faith. It is during this second phase of the purgative way that a person recognizes the maturity of others around him or her and desires to have that same sense of maturity in their own spiritual life. We might find ourselves saying, "I want to be like him." "I want to have patience like her." When we ask for that which demonstrates our maturity, we receive the opportunity to practice that maturity. In other words, we are faced with trials that give us the opportunity to mature.

Whether or not these trials have been around us all of the time and are just now noticed or whether they come our way by invitation of the life we seek is not really relevant. The truth of the matter is that they come and that we recognize them. If we pray for patience we will get the "opportunity" to use patience. If we pray for humility, we will face the "opportunity" to be humbled in order to become humble. Trials are the experience of the one who seeks to mature in faith.

It is in the issues of faith and trust that one can see the natural progression of a maturing faith from childhood and adolescence to adulthood.

> The tasks are the transcending of juvenile religiosity and adolescent religious speculation. Both behaviors are developmentally proper at a certain stage; both represent spiritual growth up to a point and both respond to human needs. The child attempts by cultic faith to manage the fear of life by attempting to control

God with good works; the adolescent uses curiosity and rational analysis to control the divine by deciding what God can and must do. We have also seen that the experience of these developmental stages must be transformed in order to perdure in a mature spiritual life. The child's cultic works become the good deeds of charity; the adolescent's questioning becomes a reverent philosophy and theology. Unfortunately, both good works and speculation can provide a camouflage for those who choose not to mature, so that they become trapped in their own works or ideas (Groeschel, 1984, pp. 120-121).

The maturation of a childhood (not necessarily a childlike) faith to a faith of adulthood is accomplished in large part through the facing of the trials of life. While it is natural for a child to try to control God and allay his or her fear of the unknown and the uncontrollable by doing so, it is the trials of life that force one to decide between a more mature faith that does not need to control God in order to know the peace of God and the other path of fanatical belief that needs by its nature to force acquiescence in order to validate itself. The second choice leads to a permanent attachment to a childhood faith of "fanaticism and chronic uncertainty" (Groeschel, 1984, p. 121).

The development of faith is the development of "belief plus actions" which is a good description of faith. It is the "assurance" of that which we hope for and the "certainty" of what we do not see (Hebrews 11:1). Faith is essential to human existence since all of us exist in a realm of incomplete knowledge. Since we do not know everything at once (as does God), we must act on what we believe to be true, retaining the right to alter our beliefs as 1) our experience dictates is necessary, and 2) as we grow in our understanding of our faith in God.

A simple example of this would be as follows. I parked my truck in the parking lot when I came to class. I believe that it is still in the parking lot and will be there when my class is over and I leave to return home. I am acting on that belief. However, when I go to the parking lot after my class is finished and observe that my truck is not there and there is broken glass on the ground where my truck was parked, I change my beliefs. I believe that someone has broken into my truck and stolen it. I call the authorities and act according to my new (changed) belief. This is a simple philosophical example of practical existentialism.

When it comes to our faith in God, it, too, changes as we grow spiritually. The changes include our understanding of God and our acceptance of the work of God in our lives for our spiritual formation. Benedict Groeschel describes the changes in our faith in God in this way:

> A single example may clarify the distinction between analogous and apophatic faith. It is revealed that God is a living, personal God. The notion we share as human beings of a human person is therefore applied to God as an analogy. It is a useful analogy which every child and adolescent can comprehend, although the young adolescent, newly capable of abstract thought, will do better than the child for whom God is an old man, the Ancient of Days. The theological student will go much further, remove the anthropomorphisms, and come to the most sublime and unlimited notion of person. The theologian can examine the concept of person, and the Scripture and dogma related to the analogy, and proceed to an almost limitless refinement especially as psychology refines its definition of person.
>
> Then the student or theologian grows silent in inner prayer and experiences a mysterious relationship with and knowledge of God. The individual experience goes beyond all concepts of person. God becomes not less than person nor more than person but beyond

person, as we understand the term (Groeschel, 1984, p. 123).

As we grow through different stages of faith, we may very well move from a faith knowledge based on analogy to an apophatic faith. The traditional views of kataphatic faith and apophatic faith should have another category added that includes a larger portion of Christians on the faith development journey. That category would be "eclecto-phatic" as many Christians are caught using both kataphatic and apophatic faith in one form or another.

The development of faith in the second phase of the purgative way is the foundational development of the human soul for faith serves as the bedrock of our relationship with God. It is by grace we are saved *through faith*, and that is not of our own doing, but it is a gift from God (Ephesians 2:8). The changes in our faith in God are a gift from God and can be received as such. Adrian Van Kaam, the noted Dutch theologian and professor of spiritual formation says:

> Faith in the daily call to formation, and fidelity to its mystery, grant us the flexibility we need to respond to formative life directives that may unpredictably come our way. When we live in anticipation of unexpected manifestations of the mystery of formation, we live in readiness for anything that may happen to us. Formative directives may influence our life in ways we never expected. What counts is the abiding awareness of being called communally, personally, and continually to ongoing foundational formation (Van Kaam, 1989, p. 210).

It is important to note that during the second stage of the purgative way, the stage of faith development, the Christian who is on this journey will find his or her anxieties continuing to decline and his or her sense of peace and freedom on the rise. Throughout the forward motion in faith development that defines this stage of the purgative way a general rise in the peace that comes from God's presence with us and the freedom from sin that accompanies a more righteous life is experienced. While no one moves forward without some hesitations and some sliding backwards, some detours and some U-turns, it is the forward motion of faith development that marks this phase of the purgative way.

Third Phase

The third phase of the purgative way is the phase of trust development. In this phase the focus is trust and the experience is darkness. This darkness is not totally unlike the darkness of the dark night or nights of the soul and the dark night of the spirit, but it is not to be confused with them, either. While the nature of spiritual darkness is the same in almost all contexts, the darkness that is at work in the dark night(s) of the soul and the dark night of the spirit is different in some very important ways which will be examined later. The trust that is the focus of this third phase of the purgative way is the "metanoia" of fear or anxiety. This term is used more in the psychological sense than the theological sense.

In theology the term "metanoia" is used to denote repentance or the changing of one's mind. In psychology, the "mind-changing" is considered to be a healing of a significant sort that usually follows a psychotic episode. The key to understanding the use of the term in a psychological context is that the "breakdown" and change are thought to be useful and healing rather than an experience to be avoided. This type of "mind-changing" although difficult is something to be desired and is, in fact, needed for true health to be present in the human soul.

In spiritual formation, the term relates to the necessary change in one's mind from the influence which fear and anxiety exert upon our thinking and acting to the influence of trust in God and the role that trust plays in the motivation of our thoughts and actions. **Trust is the "healing replacement" for**

anxiety. It makes sense, then, that spiritual darkness, or the perceived absence of God, would be the experience of one moving through this final phase of the purgative way. It is in this phase that a person desires to commit his or her whole life to God. The sense is one of wanting God to control (motivate) the entirety of one's life.

A former pastor of mine had a poster hanging in his living room that described this experience for me. On the left-hand side of the poster the background was very bright yellow. In the center of the poster a jagged line ran from top to bottom and formed the central border for both sides of the poster. The right-hand side of the poster was completely black. On the left hand side of the poster were these words: "Walking in faith is a matter of taking one more step into the darkness, knowing that when your foot comes down, there will be light."

This experience of darkness is calling us to trust in the presence of God and overcome our anxieties. The anxieties that we have are normally centered around our own illusion of control in our lives. We are afraid of what God may ask us to do, or to give up, or where God might ask us to go. On one side is our fear of turning over the control of our lives and on the other side is the growing recognition of the peace and freedom of a God who cares for us more than we could possibly know. It is a significant moment in the spiritual growth of any Christian and is often accompanied by parallel understandings.

It is often in this phase that a call to ministry is heard. It is noteworthy that many believe that this call is to some form of full-time Christian service such as the ordained ministry. While it is a call to a level of commitment that lets the presence of God be a greater motivation than one's own anxieties, it may not be a call to ordained service in the church. This confusion is understandable when it is recognized that many people who have not had a lot of experience in their relationship with God will often think that the only form of total commitment is to the ordained ministry. It is during this time in the maturation of the

Christian that a spiritual friend or guide can be most helpful. Once a person passes through this phase and from the purgative way to the illuminative way, the companionship of a spiritual guide or friend will help prevent a lot of trouble.

All Christians are called to ministry of one sort or another. The ministry to which we are called is in general terms a ministry to God by living in such a way that we fulfill God's will for our lives and further the work of the kingdom of God. It is a ministry to which all Christians are called by the nature of what a mature spiritual relationship with God entails. Trusting God and releasing our anxieties is essential to moving forward in spiritual growth. The resulting "feelings" are often quite noteworthy. John Wesley had his heart "strangely warmed." Others have described the feeling as one of being washed with love. Still others speak of being "filled" with the Spirit of God. Wesleyans have called it sanctification. Pentecostals have termed it the "baptism" with the Holy Spirit. However it is termed, it is an experience that marks a major transition in one's spiritual formation. It is the movement from the purgative way to the illuminative way.

The Illuminative Way

The second of the three ways is termed the illuminative way. It is known as a way of spiritual development in many of the world's great religions. It will here be considered in its specifically Christian context. It can be well described in this way:

> At the end of the darkness, when the level of anxiety has finally fallen below the individual's degree of peace and trust, when driven need is substantially less compelling than the freedom of the person, a new experience begins, which, in most spiritually oriented religions, is known as "enlightenment" or "illumination." The latter term used by Augustine to name the middle phase of the spiritual journey has

become conventional in Christianity (Groeschel, 1984, p. 136).

The focus of the first phase of illumination is the zeal that accompanies being set free from our illusions of control and the bondage of our anxieties. The experience is one of joy and light. The light is God's light and not our own. The joy is God's gift to those who recognize the presence of God and find in it a greater motivation for their life and actions than they found in their own anxieties. This phase is a time of recognizing the presence of God more easily and enjoying it more completely.

Thomas Merton describes the illuminative way:

Call it faith, call it (at a more advanced stage) contemplative illumnation, call it the sense of God or even mystical union: all these are different aspects and levels of the same kind of realization: the awakening to a new awareness of ourselves in Christ, created in Him, redeemed by Him, to be transformed and glorified in and with Him.

This "loving knowledge" which sees everything transfigured "in God," coming from God and working for God's creative and redemptive love and tending to fulfillment in the glory of God, is a contemplative knowledge, a fruit of living and realizing faith, a gift of the Spirit (Merton, 1973, pp. 175-76).

There are some challenges in the illuminative way. It is during this time in one's Christian spiritual formation that pride and exuberance can overshadow the true humility and purpose for the Christian life. Without a more mature spiritual friend, guide, or community of faith, a person can go astray at best and wreak havoc both within and without the Christian community at worst. The experience of freedom and the change in one's life of prayer can urge one to misunderstand the purpose of the freedom and the power that comes from the joy that accompanies the illuminative way.

It is during the early stages of the illuminative way that Christians often find a new zeal for sharing their discoveries with others and even encouraging others to join them. The problem is that most Christians in the early stages of the illuminative way know only how they, themselves, got there and wanting others to experience the same new freedom and joy in the presence of God, try to help others have the same experience that they believe brought them to this place.

The story is told of an old man who lived out at the edge of a small town in the hills. Having once been a fervent Christian, he had given up his faith and turned on God after the tragic deaths of his wife and children. The local church held a brush arbor meeting each year in the clearing beyond this man's house. Each evening the dutiful Christians of that church would walk past this man's house on the way to and from the meetings. The old man would take advantage of the opportunity to sit in his rocking chair on his front porch and chide, tease, and hurl insults at those who still had faith as they would pass by both going to and coming from the meeting.

This same story happened year after year. One night after the meeting had started, the old man became thirsty and walked from his porch across the road to get a drink from his well. As he was reaching for the bucket, he slipped, toppled over into the well and fell to the bottom. The water in the well was not deep, but he could not escape since the moss on the sides of the well would not allow him a firm foothold or hand grasp. The water was just deep enough that if he stood on his tiptoes and remained very still, he could tilt his head back, keep his nose out of the water and breathe. That night he heard the sermon that the preacher was preaching in the clearing beyond his home in a way he had never heard it before. He was motivated to re-examine his life and he accepted the new life offered by God in Christ.

When the meeting was finished, the people filed back past the house and for the first time in years found that the old man was not on the porch to insult them. Many thought little of it, but a few others wondered what had happened. They looked around, saw the well and wondered. They walked over to the well saw the old man at the bottom and quickly threw a rope down to hoist him up. After he was rescued, he relayed his experience to them and they all rejoiced. It soon became the talk of the town. Eveyone was pleased.

As time went by, new people would move to town and the church people would have to advise them not to go past the home of this old man who was now a fervent Christian, for if they went that way, he would meet them in front of his house, ask them if they were saved. If they said no, he would ask them if they would like a drink of water, take them to his well and push them in! After all, that is where he found the truth.

The illuminative way is a time of relating to God in more than an historical manner. The prayer that leads one into this way is contemplative in nature rather than meditative in nature. More will be said about this later, but for now it is important to know that this is a significant change.

> Prayer changes and certainly becomes easier. Previously meditation had been largely an inner soliloquy, that is, a measuring of self against the teachings of the Gospel; this now gives way to a gentle dialogue with Christ, characterized more by substance than by words.
>
> There is always the danger that the person at the level of affective prayer will become unfortunately a spiritual snob. The illuminative way can be dimmed by all the vices, including vanity and a touch of pride. To forestall such a development, participation in the liturgy within a parish or community is a necessary spiritual discipline (Groeschel, 1984, p. 140-41).

With the help of a spiritual friend, guide, or mature community of faith, one can move through the early stages of zeal, awe, wonder, and joy to a more complete stage of spiritual depth and "mellow out" a little. This results in a greater understanding of God's love for all people and a greater acceptance of the varieties of experiences that can lead a person to spiritual maturity. A universal experience of one who is in the illuminative way is a growing love of God and appreciation for God's presence.

Many Christians will never grow forward into the illuminative way. It is a way that is related to being spiritual and to spiritual growth which many Christians may avoid or even shun. For those who seek to grow spiritually, however, the illuminative way is a movement forward that is natural and necessary for one to be formed in the image of Christ. The second phase of the illuminative way is a growing focus on the presence of God and the experience of genuine peace.

This peace is not to be confused with a blissful state in which one does not experience problems. Quite to the contrary, the Christian who lives in the illuminative way will find not only a truly growing sense of the presence of God and the peace that passes understanding, but also a new understanding of and sense of the myriad problems that can accompany this way of spiritual living.

> In our struggles and accomplishments we recognize the power of grace and the goodness of God enabling us to do good. This recognition makes a person less judgmental, less demanding upon others and more accepting. The ability to do good easily continues to increase so that one on this way does not stop growing even if mistakes are made. It is quite possible to get off the track and even to take a bad fall, but so long as one does not turn back, progress will continue (Groeschel, 1984, p. 138).

All of this seems like a wonderful thing and something to be desired by all. It may appear that the Christian living in this way has escaped to a "trouble-free" existence. That is not the case.

> The person who does good with ease is likely to annoy many others. Those who have never started the spiritual journey will probably dismiss the whole situation as a harmless fanaticism. Those in the purgative way will be jealous even though they are good Christians and destined one day to be in the illuminative way themselves. Imprisoned as we are in the present moment with its limited perceptions, we often despise those who have accomplished precisely what we aspire to do (Groeschel, 1984, p. 138-139).

In addition to what living in the illuminative way can do to others that will result in a less enjoyable relationship with others than should be expected, the Christian who lives in this way will also become much more aware of his or her own inner turmoil. As the one who lives in the illuminative way sheds his or her "defenses of denial and rationalization," he or she will be forced to deal with the activity of the unconscious that was previously unknown to them due to their defenses.

> In return for the newly found freedom, the illuminated person faces possibilities of sin and betrayal of God which he or she never experienced. The illuminative way is not a cloudless summer day. It is a spring morning after a bad storm. Even though everything is washed clean and the sky is filled with clouds and sunlight, there are many fallen trees and an occasional live wire blocking the road (Groeschel, 1984, p. 139).

Many spiritually-minded Christians will spend the greater part of their lives in the illuminative way. Even with its added dangers and increased understanding of the possibility of sin, it is a more comfortable place to be than either the purgative way or living as a pagan. A spiritual guide, friend, or a mature community of faith is much needed for the person who is making his or her way through this part of spiritual maturity.

Spiritual pride, self-righteousness, and spiritual greed can all become problems for the one living in the illuminative way. There is the temptation to believe that one is in some way special for being chosen to fulfill a special mission. Anger may be the response to any suggestion or rebuff rather than the calm assurance of Christ and humble openness to correction that manifests itself in the more mature relationship with God. It is easy for someone newly entered into the illuminative way to be "right" but in the wrong way! (Groeschel, 1984, p. 153).

Spiritual sloth, tepidity, and spiritual paranoia are also enemies that raise their heads in new ways during the journey through the illuminative way. Those who do not understand the growth away from enlightened self-interest and toward the more restrained and Christ-centered presence of God tend to fall away and grow somewhat disinterested in continuing to be formed in the image of Christ. This is often seen among those who have grown quickly through the way of purgation and into the illuminative way through a heavily "experience-laden" journey. When the fireworks diminish, so does their interest.

Spiritual paranoia can disarm some who would otherwise move forward toward the unitive way. A good deal of true discernment is often required in order to properly diagnose and address this malady.

> St. Ignatius Loyola, a master of discernment and eminent spiritual psychologist, cast his critical eye on the many people he knew in the illuminative way and formulated some very good rules for diagnosing what in modern terms might be called "spiritual paranoia," which he called an "evil spirit." St. Ignatius noticed in some fairly fervent people a tendency to get involved in projects which troubled them or interfered with others' spiritual growth. He maintained that if a project were really good, it would contain nothing

contrary to God's will or to the soul's welfare. He noted that it is an evil spirit who suggests projects in harmony with the highest spiritual aspirations but also dependent on self-will or self-aggrandizement. Gradually through complacency, presumption, or disguised ambition in the form of excessive rigor or austerity, the project becomes an expression of self-love. Little by little a person's hard-won progress is lost and defenses are rebuilt. If called abruptly to account, the person trapped by the evil spirit can make an excellent defense: The person might explain, for example, that he or she is now an advanced person, having passed successfully through periods of trial and temptation, and is quite beyond the childish vice of self-love and self-will. And the person did indeed once advance beyond these obstacles, but has now unknowingly recreated them all (Groeschel, 1984, p. 155).

Growth during the illuminative way has all of the ups and downs of spiritual growth during any of the three ways. The positive experiences of the illuminative way vastly outweigh the negatives, even though the negatives seem more and more apparent the further one goes.

A growing love of justice is one of the positive experiences of the illuminative way. While those in the illuminative way sometimes suffer the injustice of others due to their envy, they also experience a heightened sense of justice. They are more fair and giving than others and by their changing and new nature are sometimes prone to lose sight of the fact that we live amongst a great deal of misunderstanding and wickedness. They may choose to remain quiet in the face of injustice and are among those who stand in need of learning to express truth in love and establish a just presence in the world.

One of the positive recognitions of the illuminative way is the utter poverty and dependence upon God in which Christians exist. In the second phase of the illuminative way this dependence brings about a quiet and humble recognition of the identification we have with the poor and those that mourn. Those living in the illuminative way grow toward a greater and greater identification with God and with the suffering of Christ. Although the center of this suffering during the illuminative way is found primarily in the mental-emotional dimension of the human being, it does not intend to rest there forever, nor can it. The suffering is too great for the mind to bear. Intellect and reason cannot make sense of such suffering. This recognition spurs further spiritual maturity even as those in the illuminative way open their hearts to the suffering of God and the suffering of humanity.

The peace that is increasingly experienced in the illuminative way is not a peace that acquiesces to the suffering around us and accepts some sense of our never being able to do enough about it so we will "let God take care of it." It is instead a peace that passes our under-standing of why it exists and how we can alleviate it. It is a peace that helps us to understand that God's own self is not loved enough by us. It is a peace that comes from being more fully in the presence of God in spite of our growing recognition that we do not deserve to be there. It is a peace that is built foursquare upon the grace and love of God. It is a peace that is sustained beyond our powers of reasoning, by the love of God that "draws" us toward union rather than the power of logic to "drive" us toward a more perfect relationship with God.

This difference between being "drawn" and being "driven" is the exact difference described by Dr. Frankl as the difference in motivation between the human spiritual dimension and the mental-emotional dimension. In Christian spiritual formation, one is drawn on toward the "prize of the high calling of Christ" rather than forced forward through the objections and discontent of the selfish nature. The old nature that was motivated mostly by our own anxieties and fears is now giving way to the new nature that exists in the love and peace of the presence of God. When one is living in true contemplation, one becomes ready to enter the final way of union with God.

The Unitive Way

The unitive way, like old age, is not for sissies! It is, however, the final way of preparation for union with God, which is entirely a gift of God's own giving. Everything that happens previous to union with God is like negative numbers on the numbers scale. It is a preparation for the way we were created to be. As such, it is guided by God's presence and is different for different people. It is as personal and individual as each human being, yet there are, in general, stages that can be identified and universally examined for clarity and further understanding during this time of spiritual maturity and preparation.

Mystics like St. Bonaventure, St. Teresa of Avila, and St. John of the Cross have written about the unitive way and sought to describe their understandings of this time of preparation as have many others. This description should be taken as more of an explanation than a guide. As an explanation, it will seek to establish generalities while at the same time speaking of things that are highly personal. Union with God is as unique and individual as are the human beings who expereince it. At the same time, union with God is universally available to any who would seek the presence of God with a heart that is made pure in purgation, a mind that is freed from the bondage of self-centeredness in illumination and a soul that is humbly honoring God by being fully present with God in the world.

The unitive way consists of two phases. The first is a phase of quiet contemplation. In fact, the entrance into the unitive way is marked by the movement of a Christian into a prayer life relationship with God that is contemplative instead of meditative. The second phase is a time of complete contemplative absorption. The difference is between acquired contemplation and infused contemplation. The difference is significant and has a psychological as well as a spiritual understanding. The difference will be noted later as when we focus on the difference between the dark night(s) of the soul and the dark night of the spirit.

Adolphe Tanquerey says that acquired contemplation "is, at bottom, nothing more than a simplified affective prayer" (Tanquerey, 1930, p. 605-606). Benedict Groeschel goes on to state that this "may be defined as contemplation in which the simplification of our intellectual and affective acts is the result of our own activity aided by grace" (Groeschel, 1984, p. 161). Infused contemplation is a total and complete gift from God. It is a period of receiving the full union with God that one moves toward "the complete overcoming of the normal psychological processes of the person" (Groeschel, 1984, p. 161). This second and final phase goes by more than one name. It is called ecstatic union or the spiritual marriage or total contemplative absorption.

Phase One

In the first phase of the unitive way is the time of complete contemplation that leads to an experience that is called the dark night of the soul(s). The entrance is marked by:

... a change of emphasis, an increase of one phenomenon and a concurrent decrease of another, as so many developmental changes take place. During the experience of contemplative meditation, or prayer of simplicity, those at the end of illumination experience more and more episodes of contemplation quite beyond their own powers. Like the sparks or flashes of awareness of God they experienced long ago at the beginning of the journey, these experiences of awareness are not so much overpowering as they are mentally captivating. Acts of quiet recollection may precede and follow them. But these acts are obviously much more voluntary than the moment of quiet contemplation. The questions which suddenly confront the person are: Am I willing to surrender to and cherish these moments of intense awareness of the presence of God and am I willing to reinforce them by a life of habitual virtue and generous self-giving? This is not a new problem, but there is a special urgency about it. It is important to note that subjectively these states are very different from pathological states of self-alienation. There is no psychological conflict that one is escaping from. There is no real interference with duty, no lack of understanding of others. Quite the opposite: There is an openness to a presence quite beyond oneself – a presence of God which brings with it a new openness to the presence of other people and of other things.

As the experience of this new and simple acquired contemplation takes over and the affective prayer of the illuminative way decreases, there emerges a time of simple union with God (Groeschel, 1984, pp. 163-164).

This experience of simple union with God in the quiet affective prayer of acquired contemplation leads one to the experience of the dark night(s) of the soul. There may be more than one experience of a dark night of the soul as it is the shedding of any dependence upon our "religious" activity in the mental-emotional dimension of the human life. During this phase of the unitive way, God withdraws any and all awareness of God's presence with us in the mental-emotional dimension. While in truth God is still present with us, we have no ability to recognize that presence in the mental-emotional dimension of life. It feels and seems to us that God is no longer present.

The first lesson to be learned is that contemplation is a kind of darkness for all our powers, even the intellect; thus this simple relation to God, unlike the contemplative meditation of the illuminative way, goes beyond our conscious awareness of the truths of faith. It is a gift given in a Dark Night (Groeschel, 1984, p. 170).

It is amazing how we can rest our belief upon our own thoughts and feelings instead of centering it in the reality of God. The dark night(s) of the soul is a time of ridding our lives of belief that is based on anything within us; anything that is of our own doing. It feels as if God is gone. When we try to think or reason our way through the experience, we find that there is nothing there upon which we can hang our beliefs or our trust in God. In such a time, it is important to have a spiritual friend or guide who will not allow one to settle for something less than moving through this experience. In fact, some consideration should be given to the advice of those that encourage us to have at least two different spiritual directors, one who is tough and another who is gentle and understanding, as it is difficult (although not impossible) for one person to fulfill the same role in both capacities.

One who is passing into union with God and moving throuh a dark night of the soul should continue to live the Christian life. He or she should continue to pray and serve and study and share even though the feelings of the presence of God are absent. It is through this absence that he or she will continue to be prepared to be in union with God, who truly is God, instead of a lesser version of God in some way pared down to fit a faith that rests on our own understandings or feelings of God's presence. The reason that there may be more than one dark night of the soul is that there may be more than one way in which the person who is passing through this preparation is trusting in something less than God in order to be in God's presence.

The dark night of the soul is also called the dark night of the senses. Benedict Groeschel references St. John of the Cross using the analogy of wood and fire to describe this experience.

> For the sake of further clarity in this matter, we ought to note that this purgative and loving knowledge or divine light we are speaking of, has the same effect on the soul that fire has on a log of wood. The soul is purged and prepared for union with the divine light just as the wood is prepared for transformation into the fire. Fire, when applied to wood, first dehumidifies it, dispelling all moisture and making it give off any water it contains. Then it gradually turns the wood black, makes it dark and ugly, and even causes it to emit a bad odor. By drying out the wood, the fire brings to light and expels all those ugly and dark accidents which are contrary to fire. Finally, by heating and enkindling it from without, the fire transforms the wood into itself and makes it as beautiful as it is itself. Once transformed, the wood no longer has any activity or passivity of its own, except for its weight and its quantity, which is denser than the fire (Groeschel, 1984, p. 173).

Once through the first phase of the unitive way, the focus is upon the quiet ecstasy of the presence of God and the experience is that of having lost all of one's defenses. Without leaning on one's own understanding, the relationship one has with God is deeper and richer and purer than ever before. It is during this time that the prayer of full union is the act of worship for the Christian moving through the unitive way into full union with God.

Phase Two

The dark night(s) of the soul is(are) the time(s) of preparation for an even deeper and more transcendent preparation experience; the dark night of the spirit. This second phase of the unitive way is led by the presence of God in an even greater sense than one perceived in the dark night(s) of the soul (senses). The dark night of the spirit is similar but more inclusive than the dark night(s) of the soul. It occurs in the most inclusive of all of the human dimensions. It is entered as God withdraws all awareness of God's presence from the spiritual dimension in the human life. Since this dimension is the largest of the human dimensions and includes all of the psychic (mental-emotional) dimension and the somatic dimension but transcends them, it is also the most inclusive of the human dimensions.

When God withdraws all awareness of God's presence from the spiritual dimension in the human life, there is nothing to which we can turn for relief. There are no practices, conscious, preconscious, or unconscious that can remain unexamined by God. This dark night of the spirit closes every false door to the presence of God and positions the Christian toward the only place from which relief and life can come – God's own self. Again, Groeschel cites St. John of the Cross as he seeks to describe this phenomenon.

> He (St. John of the Cross) paints a picture of extremely advanced souls undergoing purification by periods of darkness and aridity, or plunged into utter darkness convinced that God has abandoned them forever. He lists certain imperfections of persons at this level suggesting that the "stains of the old man still linger in the spirit." The desire for absolute purity may be a difficult concept to grasp, but in *The Living Flame of Love* he clarifies the problem when he speaks of memory, intellect, and will as vast caverns of the soul, as deep and empty as what they are destined to possess. He points out that at this level "any little thing which adheres in them will burden and bewitch them" and yet when the caverns are empty and pure,

the thirst and hunger for God is overwhelming and fills the soul with pain. When the purification we have described has taken place and the divine has not yet communicated itself in perfect union, there is experienced an impatient love so that the person must be filled or die. Thus we find here a darkness that is a reaction to imperfection and absolute desire (Groeschel, 1984, p. 185).

When one moves through the dark night of the spirit and awaits the transforming union that results, life becomes the prayer of passive union which results in infused contemplation. This completeness is the union of wills that takes place between God's will and the Christian's will. Evelyn Underhill describes this entrance into full union this way:

Coming first to the evidence of the mystics themselves, we find that in their attempts towards describing the Unitive Life they have recourse to two main forms of symbolic expression; both very dangerous, and liable to be misunderstood, both offering ample opportunity for harsh criticism to hostile investigators of the mystic type. We find also, as we might expect from our previous encounters with the symbols used by contemplatives and ecstatics, that these two forms of expression belong respectively to mystics of the transcendent-metaphysical and of the intimate-personal type: and that their formulae, if taken alone, appear to contradict one another.

1) The metaphysical mystic, for whom the Absolute is impersonal and transcendent, describes his final attainment of that Absolute as *deification,* or the utter transmutation of the self in God. 2) The mystic for whom intimate and personal communion has been the mode under which he best apprehended Reality, speaks of the consummation of this communion, its

perfect and permanent form, as the *Spiritual Marriage* of his soul with God (Underhill, 1911, p. 415).

She goes on to explain that these expressions of the depth of the unitive way and the infused contemplation that accompanies it can best be understood pyschologically as well as spiritually.

> . . . the Unitive State is essentially a state of free and filial participation in Eternal Life. The capital marks of the state itself are (1) a complete absorption in the interests of the Infinite, under whatever mode It is apprehended by the self; (2) a consciousness of sharing Its strength, acting by Its authority, which results in a complete sense of freedom, and invulnerable serenity, and usually urges the self to some form of heroic effort or creative activity; (3) the establishment of the self as a "power for life," a centre of energy, an actual parent of spiritual vitality in other men.
>
> From the point of view of the pure psychologist, what do the varied phenomena of the Unitive Life, taken together, seem to represent? He would probably say that they indicate the final and successful establishment of that higher form of consciousness which has been struggling for supremacy during the whole of the Mystic Way. The deepest, richest levels of human personality have now attained to light and freedom. The self is remade, transformed, has at last unified itself; and with the cessation of stress power has been liberated for new purposes (Underhill, 1911, p. 416).

From the point of view of spirituality, she writes:

> The mystic, I think, would acquiesce in these descriptions, so far as they go: but he would probably translate them into his own words and gloss them with an explanation which is beyond the power and province of psychology. He would say that his long-

sought correspondence with Transcendental Reality, his union with God, has now been finally established: that his self, though intact, is wholly penetrated – as a sponge by the sea – by the Ocean of Life and Love to which he has attained. "I live, yet not I but God in me." He is conscious that he is now at length cleansed of the last stains of separation, and has become, in a mysterious manner, "that which he beholds" (Underhill, 1911, pp. 416-417).

This transforming union is the purpose of the spiritual journey and the apex of spiritual maturity. It is accomplished not by the efforts of the Christian, though it takes much effort. It is solely a gift of the grace of God granted by God when God knows that the Christian is adequately prepared for the fullness of life that God first imagined for all of God's creation. The driving force in spiritual maturity is not the effort of the Christian that is put into the process of preparation. It is rather the movement of the nature of the relationship that the Christian has with God. It is found in prayer.

The Place of Prayer in the Three Ways

Movement in the three ways is related to the type of prayer that is lived by the Christian. There are in general seven types of prayer that represent the life of the Christian related to God. These various types of prayer can be understood in some measure and practiced by the Christian. They exist as growth in one's relationship with God and draw the Christian forward into greater dimensions of spiritual maturity. They are petition, meditation, meditative-contemplation, contemplative-meditation, contemplation, the prayer of full union, and the prayer of passive union. The final two types are actually specialized forms of contemplation in that they are focused on a particular outcome that leads to full union. In full union, contemplation becomes the norm for communication between God and the Christian.

It is most important to note that prayer is what moves the Christian forward in his or her spiritual formation. While various experiences can and do make tremendous impressions in the life of the Christian, it is in prayer that our truly dynamic relationship with God is defined. For most Christians, that relationship is begun with petition.

Petition
Petition is the prayer that for most Christians represents the nature of the initial relationship with God. It is a matter of asking God for things. Those things are varied according to the understanding of the world and of one's perceived needs. Petition is not only the initial form of prayer, it is also the most pervasive form of prayer. As a type of prayer, petition stays with the Christian throughout his or her journey in the spiritual life. Even though the Christian will move on to practice other forms of prayer, petition will remain a constant in the life of the Christian. What is petitioned for by the Christian will change, perhaps dramatically, as the Christian matures.

In the beginning stages of the Christian life, the purgative way, a Christian will ask for help to overcome old habits, to change desires and even, at times, to change circumstances, so that a better, more Christ-like life can be lived. At several points in the purgative way, a Christian may ask for things without any concern as to whether or not those things that are asked for are actually God's will for the Christian. The largest influence in the life of the Christian in the early stages of the purgative way is the desire that the Christian has to alleviate things that are not wanted. It is still the Christian's own understanding of what is wanted and not wanted that takes precedence over a small, but growing recognition of God's will.

As the Christian grows spiritually, petition takes on more and more the desire to ask for those things that God is wanting for the Christian. In the unitive way, petition is simply a matter of joining with God in desiring and asking for the will of God to be fulfilled in the Kingdom of God. The specifics of such prayers are as unique and individual as are the lives of those who are in union with God.

Along the way of purgation, a Christian will desire to know more about God and to be even more so, the person that God has created him or her to be. To know more about God, one will read the Bible more, avail one's self of the opportunities to hear what others know about God through worship, preaching and teaching, and will discover that another type of prayer is necessary to know God better. That type of prayer is meditation.

Meditation

Meditation is a type of prayer that is practiced by many religions and even by the non-religious it is seen as a thought-process that will help grant one a better way of life. For that reason, it is important for us to consider it within the context of the practice of the Christian faith.

Christian meditation can best be described as "thinking about the thoughts of God." It is historic in nature in that a person who is engaged in Christian meditation will be thinking about thoughts that God has already had. Christian meditation is:

> A very human endeavor with steps and techniques; it requires much human energy and initiative (Groeschel, 1984, p. 141).

Christian meditation is much more than an exercise in relaxation, although relaxation may be involved in order to heighten the focus necessary in meditation. A Christian will focus on a subject (a thought that God has already had) such as love, or peace, or goodwill and will aim the mind at using its powers of memory, logic, and rationalism in the highest sense to grow forward and be molded in the image of God in our thinking. This will, in turn, change our actions to be more like the actions of God given our circumstances.

In this way, meditation is a very historic event. Even though the mind is using thoughts that have already been entertained, it is bringing them together in ways that bring new insight into the subject of focus and making application of those new insights in the living of one's life. Meditation provides one with a powerful way to continue to purge one's life of those things that do not belong there and institute in one's life those thoughts and activities that are more Christ-like. One could meditate well beyond his or her lifetime and never exhaust the available subjects for focus in meditation. Reading and study of the Bible provide an ever-enlarging circle of foci for meditation as the essence and nature of God is revealed through the scriptures.

Contemplation

Contemplation is best understood as "thinking the thoughts of God with God." It is "real time" rather than historic in nature. It is an active, dynamic participation in the thinking process between a Christian and God. It is most usually not arrived at in total or all at once. It is, instead, experienced in parcels that grow in duration and depth as a Christian grows forward spiritually.

The first experiences of contemplation are more correctly known as **meditative-contemplation**. While meditating, a Christian will experience moments where God has joined the conversation. This provides a new kind of dynamic to the insight that is discovered and to the changes that are made. It is, indeed, this very transition that denotes the movement between the purgative and the illuminative ways. The recognition that God is "real" in the sense of being totally "alive now" and not just a subject of historical focus for one to meditate upon, is a life-changing recognition. Some Christians fall back into trying diligently to reproduce these moments through more intense meditation or through some careful set of exercises that they perceive preceded the revelatory nature of these new moments of contemplation. They will, however, discover that contemplation is not a human endeavor. It is a gift from God.

As one moves through the purgative way and enters the illuminative way, the life of prayer becomes more acurately described as that of **contemplative-meditation**. It is just as it is stated, a matter of how the bulk of the relationship is defined. In the earlier stages of the illuminative way there is more meditation than contemplation involved. As one moves through the illuminative way, he or she does so precisely because there is more contemplation than meditation involved in the life of prayer that defines the Christian's relationship with God.

Contemplation is recognized as the awareness of the very real presence of God and the participation of the human faculties with that presence in conversation and thought and action. The more one recognizes the infused nature of contemplation, the less he or she will try to "make" it happen and the more relaxed and open he or she will become to accepting this new way of living together with God. There is no positive connection between the work of meditation and the infused nature of contemplation. Contemplation is the antithesis to meditation and is, therefore, something that we must "let" happen rather than "make" happen.

The movement into **simple contemplation** is a movement that is as unobtrusive as the previous movement from meditation to contemplation was dynamic. This simple movement into contemplation as a way of life in one's relationship with God is the point of transition from the illuminative way to the unitive way. While there are many other things going on, they are indeed the result of, or the harvest of, those seeds that have been planted and nurtured in the movement into participation in the presence of God that is fostered in the contemplative life. It is the pure nature of being united to God that draws the Christian forward during this time.

Prayer of Full Union

The relaxed nature of simple contemplation belies the depth of pain and frustration that accompanies the movement through the dark night(s) of the soul and the dark night of the spirit. Both of these times of growth are the continuation of the preparation of the Christian for union with God. Following the dark night(s) of the soul there is a time of the loss of all defenses as the Christian experiences a greater depth (or width) of the contemplative life. It is during this time that contemplation has accomplished its purpose in the psychic and somatic dimensions of the human being. In this time the prayer of full union becomes the focus of the spiritual life. There is a true longing for full union that can only be satisfied by the continuous and complete experience of union. There is, however, another dimension in the human being in need of final preparation, i.e. the spiritual dimension.

Prayer of Passive Union

The dark night of the spirit is the preparation for the infusion of contemplation in the spiritual dimension of the human being. Moving through this experience is the direct answer to the prayer of full union. There are no words to describe the fullness of this experience although the saints have tried down through the centuries to help us understand the reality of this part of the unitive way. Spiritual marriage, ecstasy, glorious union, are all terms that have been used to describe the result of the movement through the dark night of the spirit. There is a transforming sense of union with God that awaits the answer to the next prayer which is the prayer of passive union. This prayer is lived in the full recognition that infused contemplation is truly a gift from God which is given in God's time.

We should keep in mind that we are talking about complete human beings that are moving through this experience of Christian spiritual formation known as the three ways. The danger is to somehow so compartmentalize the wholeness of the human being that we devalue some dimension of human existence. Such is not the case in this understanding of the three ways. The preparation for healing and wholeness known as union with God involves a very "high" valuation of all of the dimensions of the human being.

The next step in understanding how the use of Franklian psychology helps in the establishment of a meaning matrix for Christian spiritual growth is the understanding of the place of psychology in Christian spiritual formation in general. No one has approached this subject more completely or more thoroughly than Benedict Groeschel.

In the next chapter we will examine the place of psychology in spiritual formation and in Christian spiritual formation in particular.

CHAPTER VI
CURRENT APPLICATIONS OF PSYCHOLOGY TO THE THREE WAYS

Psychology has always been related to the understanding of the development of human beings overall and to their spiritual development as well. Long before there was a discipline in the field of science, there was due consideration given to the ability of humans to think, feel and reason.

Psychological Overlay
The application of psychology certainly predates the establishment of the discipline.
With the possible exception of child-rearing, the study of a person's relationship with God is the oldest and most integrated of all human endeavors. Almost every great culture has given rise not only to popular religiosity but also to a spirituality arising from popular attempts to court the divine powers by prayer, or to understand them through the study of signs. Besides the religions which grew out of God's revelation to Abraham, several important spiritual movements have flourished including Buddhism, Hinduism, and the Graeco-Roman philosophical religion, which found its greatest expression in Plato. These movements are generally characterized by presenting a pattern of spiritual progress. This is the most important element shared with Christian spirituality (Groeschel, 1984, p. 13).
With the development of psychology as a discipline in the field of human sciences, the application of human development to spiritual development seemed to be a natural movement. However, the steps of human development were applied without

a serious attempt to analyze the stages of spiritual development written about by the great mystics of the past.

This does not mean that the stages of human development are unimportant in one's understanding and practice of spiritual development. Quite to the contrary, these stages can be very helpful in understanding the psychological makeup of the persons moving through spiritual development to spiritual maturity. The development of trust, autonomy and initiative are important to the early years of life. The development in early adolescence of creativity and individuality will mature into the generosity and altruistic care of adulthood that provides a solid foundation for the next generation.

The transition from adolescence to adulthood can create some enduring problems. In more agrarian societies this transition may last for a very short period of time. In less agrarian societies, where the movement into an independent, self-supporting, and self-directed lifestyle is delayed, many problems can arise. These include:

> ... aimlessness, boredom, indulgence in pleasure and resultant self-hate or guilt, self-destructive tendencies and several other psychological mishaps, especially for those who have suffered scars in childhood (Groeschel, 1984, p. 47).

Adolescence moves into adulthood with the beginnings of a stable life that fosters mutually supportive relationships, independence, self-supporting activity, and self-direction in the decisions that determine the direction of one's life. When this transition is made successfully, intimacy is the result. When it is not made successfully, isolationism is the result.

Midlife becomes the time of choice. It is during this time that choices are made that relate to the rest of one's life. It can be a time of adjustment and development where some of the failed adjustments of the past can be made up for by the wise choices of this stage of development. Groeschel refers to Levinson's writings in this way:

Unreal expectations had to be resolved in the transitional stage of their thirties. Without such a resolution, the individual would live a half-life of unreality and disappointment leading to many negative personality traits, including unproductive habits, stagnation and selling out to life, or even erratic behavior, like addiction or sexual deviations (Groeschel, 1984, p. 56).

Groeschel goes on to point out that choice is of the utmost importance in the area of spiritual growth. It is of little value to study genuine religion and spirituality from the reductionistic point of view suggested by the psychodynamics of need, pleasure, or drive and power. The mystics through the centuries who have demonstrated the spiritual maturity that we study were men and women of choice.

They chose to believe what they could not see and to pursue an ideal which had nothing to do with unresolved childhood needs. Often they did this at the cost of their own lives. No modern writer in the field of psychology and religion has expressed the need for choice and decision more effectively than Viktor Frankl. His early work, *Man's Search for Meaning*, is written with the passion of one who had survived torture, imprisonment, and the constant threat of arbitrary murder. The experience of life had literally become a nightmare for him. He simply had to choose what attitudes to adopt in the face of a terrible injustice perpetrated by the Nazis. The believer seldom faces such a dramatic challenge. However, the fading dream of adolescence may challenge every fiber of choice for the individual. How dramatically is this challenge of choice seen in the Gospels where Christ gradually unveils to His followers the true dimensions of the Kingdom, as well as the awesome dimensions of their inability to live up to the challenge (Groeschel, 1984, p. 56).

The next period is a time of "settling down" and a time of focus upon those things in life that have higher value. It is a time of maturity that is characterized by stability, sincerity, nobility of purpose, opportunity to express ambition, and even willingness to take risks according to Groeschel. He also points out that the Whiteheads identify the middle years as marked by the themes of personal power, care, and interiority. These are the needs to do well in one's productive endeavors: To do things that make a difference. The need to be needed and to care for others and the increased sensitivity to the self that is accompanied by a need for self-care.

The movement to late mid-life and old age has been a much studied field as of late. The movement of the baby boomers into this time of life in unprecedented numbers has been the cause of much study, most often with the hope of related financial benefit since this group of people still represents the largest and most affluent segment of society. This is a time of learning to accept oneself as he or she truly is. It is a time of physical decline and giving over to others that which we have been used to having for ourselves. According to Erikson, it is a time of "Ego integrity vs. despair." If a person clings to the fantasies of an idealized youth, he or she will experience bitterness, negativism, and overdependency on others. If this time of life welcomes the transitions that are necessary and appropriate to it, a true time of maturity and peace may ensue.

Benedict Groeschel asks five pertinent questions concerning Psychology and spirituality and offers answers that help us understand the important connection and distinctions between the two. Since some aspects of therapeutic psychology are used in the process of spiritual formation in its practical sense, it is important that we know the connection as well as the differences between the two.

The first question is: *Are psychological adjustment and spiritual development the same thing?* The answer is "no." They are related, but they are not synonymous.

> Psychological adjustment is a dynamic, ongoing process in which the individual seeks to make productive use of his or her abilities and at the same time fulfill personal needs adequately. Perfect adjustment or balance is an abstract ideal. Human adjustment is always made within realistic parameters of a situation.
>
> Spiritual development, on the other hand, is built on divine grace. God is not a psychologist and He will choose person and means of His own. . . . Spiritual development relates primarily to a person's willingness to respond openly to God, and an equal willingness to embrace the truth, at least as one knows it.
>
> As we have noted, an obvious relationship exists between psychological adjustment and spiritual growth. A good adjustment leads to an overall decline in defensiveness and anxiety, thus bringing about a better perception of reality which certainly contributes to spiritual development (Groeschel, 1984, pp. 94-95).

The second question is: *In certain religious systems obedience to a higher order of reality demands self-denial and self-sacrifice. Can such systems hold out to their adherents the possibility of self-fulfillment as it is proposed in most psychological theories?* The conflict between therapeutic psychology and the transcendent values of a revealed religion such as Christianity, Judaism, and Islam, is a very real conflict.

> The commands of a transcendent order and the exigencies of obedience to faith in a personal God are incomprehensible to those with a world vision which is either atheistic or deistic, that is, one specifically affirming an impersonal deity, like the god of Spinoza. Atheists who follow a movement that gives a quasi-

religious identity to a "divine state" are in fact better able to comprehend the need for obedience and dedication beyond oneself than those who raise the human to a quasi-divine level, as is done in secular humanism. The real question is one of dedication and commitment beyond one's own gratification, however nobly that self-seeking may be described.

A new work by Daniel Yankelovich blames a good deal of this kind of thinking on Rogers, Fromm, and especially Maslow. Yankelovich points out the existentially contradictory nature of the philosophy of self-fulfillment which has obtained in psychotherapy and throughout American culture for the past twenty years. Self-seeking, as mystics learned long ago, leads to the inevitable frustration of loneliness and isolation. We have all seen that in extreme forms found among wealthy eccentrics, the ultimate self-seeking often results in schizophrenia. Yankelovich also suggests optimistically that many young people are moving toward a new culture of commitment and a sense of the sacred (Groeschel, 1984, pp. 96-97).

This leads us to the third question which is: *Is the psychological good of the individual, therefore, irreconcilable with a higher order of values?* The answer is, "Not necessarily so." One of the results of spiritual transformation is a greater sense of altruism and a greater degree of altruistic behavior. In truth, the psychological good of the individual and the nature of the higher order of values represented in spiritual maturity are actually extremely similar and very compatible.

Spiritual transformation, contemplation, and the ultimate unity of individual and social good are concepts to which psychology is usually unwilling to extend itself – except when it is moved to deny them. Contemporary psychology, as Vitz often points out, is agnostic in its principles and atheistic in its prejudices.

Pop psychology demonstrates fewer of these biases because of the popularity of religion. However, it is an observable phenomenon that science in general, and psychology in particular, are permitted to move into theological and philosophical areas of discussion only when they are atttempting to deny the transcendent. Normally they are not allowed to approach this field of thought when, as in the present case, the only coherent answer can be found in an appeal to a Reality which encompasses both the individual and the whole of humankind. Frankl has noted the devastating effects of this prejudice on the history of modern societies; in his opinion, such thinking built the concentration camps of the Nazis (Groeschel, 1984, pp. 97-98).

The fourth question is: *In view of the widespread acceptance of selfism in therapeutic psychology, is there any hope for the adoption of spirituality or any other structure that requires self-transcendence and commitment beyond one's own pleasures and interests?* Groeschel answers this question with a hope and a warning. Unfortunately, while some have heeded the hope in the intervening two and a half decades since it was written, most have not, and the warning has rapidly become the norm.

First the hope:

This question is asked in many ways by those interested in the survival of family life, religious life, pastoral ministry, or indeed of any society where the individual finds his or her dignity going beyond mere self-interest. For several years I too have observed a small but growing trend among the postadolescent and young adult population toward commitment and altruism. Such trends seem frequently to be reactions against the boredom of hedonism (Groeschel, 1984, p. 98).

Then the warning:

While many other signs indicate that the young are rejecting the culture of selfism, middle-aged people often fail to understand this rejection of an apparent freedom that was won less than a generation ago. They remember days of excessive control and repression. It is not so long ago that many of the serious and dedicated were, at the same time, unrelated to others. The middle-aged are well aware that moral inhibition is by no means a straight road to altruism and creativity.

For a year or two, spirituality even became a fad, although I suspect this was a part of selfism. Now that the fad has subsided, people everywhere are discovering the social and communal appeal of transcendent meaning and beauty. It is very important that this interest lead to a well-informed, integrating spirituality, one that is committed to others and has a genuine sense of the sacred.

If the organized religious bodies of America fail to grasp the moment of what Yankelovich calls our first cultural revolution, they will continue to lose ground (Groeschel, 1984, pp. 98-99).

In the intervening 24 years since the publishing of this statement, the organized religious bodies of the mainstream in America have indeed continued to lose ground. Now it appears that even the "non-denominational" and "independent" religious bodies that have sprung up to fill the gap, are beginning a downhill slide themselves. The number of people identifying themselves as "unchurched" is growing. It is possible that the effects of "selfism" upon religion continue to take a terrible toll.

The fifth and final question is: *Is psychology a help in understanding spirituality?* The answer is yes, it is a help, when it is "properly and cautiously used."

Spirituality does not exist in a vacuum. It is a phase of human growth and development, albeit responding to the impetus of grace, a help that comes from beyond any human source.

A person responds to grace and revelation in a social context, and both sociology and social psychology open up great areas of understanding. A person responds with his or her personality as it has developed, with many scars and wounds; thus therapeutic psychology can be very helpful. Human beings respond in different ways at different phases of development, and therefore developmental psychology and experimental psychology can provide a good deal of insight (Groeschel, 1984, p. 99).

Psychology in the Monastery

For the last fifteen years of the twentieth century, I made regular visits to a Benedictine monastery in Atchison, Kansas, for the purpose of study and retreat. As a result I was able to become acquainted with several of the monks and brothers who were members of that monastic community. I was welcomed as a stranger and treated in the kindest of ways. I was invited to worship and eat with them on the days that I was present.

I was particularly interested in the conversations I had with one of the young monks. Michael was in his early thirties and had been in the monastery for six years. I asked him about the transitions that he had experienced and those he was still experiencing. That is when I discovered that each of the monks and brothers had a regular visit from a psychologist provided through the diocese. The purpose of the psychologist was to see that the monks and brothers continued to make healthy psychological adjustments and were able to move through the normal phases of human development.

In a very real sense, I discovered that the population of that monastery was better adjusted psychologically than were the members of my own faith community. It gave me an understanding of the role of psychology in the process of spiritual development. I asked Michael if that ever interfered with the work of spiritual formation and how the two disciplines interacted. I also visited with one of the monks who was a spiritual director about this same subject. Both of them agreed that they experienced no problems. They did say that it was most likely because the psychologist was a "believer" and a life-long Catholic who understood the fundamentals of their faith. They also said that they believed that their life in the monastery and their service in the world was much better since the inception of the psychological care.

    This experience taught me that psychology and spiritual formation can work together for the betterment of the human being. My time with the monks and brothers of the monastery was further encouragement for me to apply what I knew of the two fields together in hopes of finding a deeper and richer sense of meaning. I believe that is accomplished, at least in part, in the application of Franklian psychology to the Chrisitan spiritual formation methodology known as the three ways and the resultant meaning matrix.

CHAPTER VII
FRANKLIAN PSYCHOLOGY, THE THREE WAYS, AND THE MEANING MATRIX

Franklian psychology is particularly suited to spirituality because it recognizes the spiritual dimension of the human being. It does so without making the existence of this dimension dependent upon any particular aspect of any particular religious view. It recognizes the human spiritual dimension as part of the wholistic view of the human being.

That being said, it should be recognized that the use of Franklian psychology to better understand the methodology of Christian spiritual formation known as the three ways is quite appropriate without in any way detracting from its use to help in other forms or views of spiritual formation either within Christianity or beyond Christianity to other religious views. No special claims are made to this view that would in any way suggest that Franklian psychology is in some way specifically wedded to the Christian view. Quite to the contrary, Franklian psychology is useful in this way specifically because of its transcendent view and its pristine ability to further understand the nature of the human being through its view of human dimensional ontology.

This chapter contains the heart of my theory that by combining the use of Franklian psychology and the three ways, one can develop a meaning matrix that will lead to a better understanding of the significant transition points in Christian spiritual formation. This increased understanding can better enable Christians to move through those points of transition and further their forward growth to spiritual maturity. The following section depicts how the two are wed in order to accomplish this goal.

The Franklian Dimensional Ontology Axis

To establish the grid for the meaning matrix, we first need to establish the Franklian dimensional ontology axis. It is made up of the somatic dimension, the psychic dimension and the noetic dimension. It is on the vertical axis of the meaning matrix.

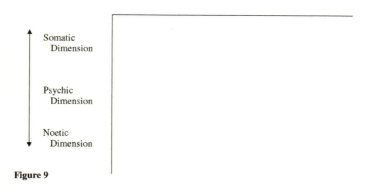

Figure 9

This axis represents the whole person. While we are focused on these three specific dimensions, they are seen as three parts of an inclusive whole. As has been stated previously, the somatic dimension is the smallest of the human dimensions. The Psychic dimension includes everything that is in the somatic dimension and yet transcends it and the noetic dimension includes everything that is in both the somatic and the psychic dimension and transcends them. As we move down the vertical axis from top to bottom, we are moving through the wholeness of the human being. It is this whole human being that experiences spiritual development.

The Spiritual Formation Axis

The horizontal axis is the spiritual formation axis. It consists of the movement of Christian spiritual formation or the three ways: The purgative way, the illuminative way and the unitive way. Movement through this axis represents the movement forward to spiritual maturity.

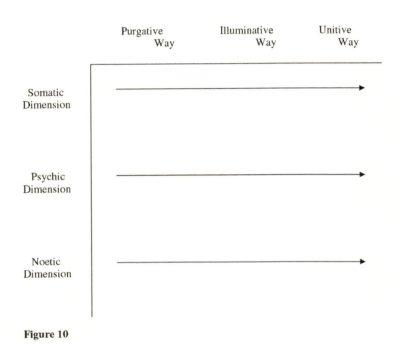

Figure 10

The spiritual formation axis includes all of the information we included in Chapter Five about the three ways. The grid represents the movement of the whole person through the process of spiritual formation. In our mind's eye, we would see the movement of the person from left to right on this grid that forms the foundation of the meaning matrix.

My contention is that the methods of meaning discovery put forth in Franklian psychology operate in meaningful ways within the different dimension of the human being at various points in one's spiritual development. While no claim is made that a certain method is used exclusively in any dimension at any point in the process of spiritual formation, I am suggesting that certain methods are used in a "primary" way in certain dimensions at certain points in the process of spiritual formation. It is this hypothesis that stands at the foundation of the formation of the meaning matrix.

Methods of Meaning Discovery in the Purgative Way

Figure 11 demonstrates the primary methods of meaning discovery that are used in the various human dimensions during the movement through the purgative way. While all three of the methods of meaning discovery are at use, the focus here is upon the primary method at use in a particular dimension during this phase of spiritual formation.

In the somatic dimension, the primary method of meaning discovery is focused around attitudinal values. The body experiences the suffering that is unavoidable when one moves into the Christian life. The movement into the Christian life is the movement through the reality and consequences of sin in general (our separation from God) and the sins in particular that manifest that separation. In this sense, the body has become the "instrument" of sin since the body is the instrument of use for the expression of existence to the world in which we live and move and have our being.

	Purgative Way	Illuminative Way	Unitive Way
Somatic Dimension	Attitudinal Values		
Psychic Dimension	Experiential Values		
Noetic Dimension	Creative Values		

Figure 11

As one is involved in the process of purgation, the body is the main point of suffering as one's life is changed from a collection of habits and actions that represent the sinfulness of being separated from God to a life that is being molded in the image of Christ. Old habits are broken. New habits are formed. The body expresses the new understanding of and commitment to the "things of God" that comes from moving through the purgative way. Even though this is considered "suffering" due to the changes that take place, the end result is often a much healthier existence biologically as well as psychologically and spiritually.

For instance, if the sin of gluttony is one of the demonstrations of one's separation from God, the body will have to face the suffering that comes from eating habits that are more in harmony with the will of God. This suffering, although very real, results in a healthier body in the end. Another example of this suffering would be in the placement of the body and its resultant suffering. When one is separated from God, one's friends and community will most likely represent that separation. The body may be adjusted to the long nights and late mornings. When one's community is changed due to the changes brought about in the Chrisian life, the body may have to suffer through the adjustments to these changes which might very well be changes in sleep and exercise as well as eating.

Change is unavoidable when one becomes a Christian. Entering the purgative way begins the formation of a Christ-like nature within us and the change is complete with the suffering that is ultimately expressed through the somatic dimension. One can not become a Christian in "thought only." The Christian life must be expressed in the thoughts, words, and deeds of a person if it is to be genuine at all. This unavoidable change requires the suffering of that dimension that expressed our existence in the world. That is the somatic dimension.

In the psychic dimension, the primary focus on the method of meaning discovery is found in experiential values. During the process of purgation, the mind of the Christian is focused on a new center! The old has passed away and the new has come. The old is the "self" centeredness of the expression of one's love while the new is the new focus for that love. The new focus is the reality of the presence of God. As one moves forward through the purgative way, the presence of God becomes an ever-greater motivator for one's thoughts, words, and deeds. This new God-centeredness is the focus of the activity of the psychic dimension.

This shifting of love from self in the center to God in the center also opens a door to the huge potential and tremendous power of love. Since in Christian understanding, God is love, this focus upon God is the very act of loving the source of love, itself. As the "imposter" (love of self) is replaced by the true focus of love, itself (God), the anxieties that accompany a life based on something less than the truth tend to lessen and are replaced by the peace and freedom that comes from being centered on the presence of God. In the purgative way, it is in the psychic dimension that God assumes the center. It is through the activity of the mind that God is believed in, accepted, and glorified (literally – brought to the center and lifted up).

The focus for meaning discovery in the noetic dimension during the purgative way is found primarily in creative values. When the human spiritual dimension is awakened to the genuinely spiritual nature of God, a new life is being created in the image of God. That image is found theologically in part (albeit, a very important part) in the reality of the existence of God as a dynamic relationship of interdependent dimensions; i.e. Father, Son, and Holy Spirit and is perceived as primarily (in the largest order) a spiritual being. "God is spirit and those that worship God must worship God in spirit and in truth" (John 4:24). Likewise, human beings are a dynamic relationship of interdependent dimensions and, we, too, are primarily (in the largest order) spiritual beings.

Previous to this "awakening" the interdependence of these dynamic dimensions is somewhat misaligned in that the psychic dimension is most often perceived as the dimension of control for the human being. Due to the reality of and the power in the act of volition, the human mind is perceived as the agent of control in the human being. Even though the mind and its functions are crucial to the life of the human being, and even though the power present in the act of volition is tremendous, indeed, the "control" that is granted to the powers of the mind is illusory at best and destructive at worst.

A large part of the activity that follows the "awakening" of a person to the Christian life is the growing understanding of the power of the human spirit and its connection to the Spirit of God. The primary activity of the noetic (spiritual) dimension during the purgative way is the ordering of a "new" life, molded in the image of Christ. The primarily spiritual nature of this entire endeavor is a growing awareness on the part of the Christian who is moving through to spiritual maturity that the human life is primarily a spiritual life. It is the simple and growing understanding of the transcendence of the human dimensions and the realization of the reality that the human being is primarily a spiritual being.

Methods of Meaning Discovery in the Illuminative Way

The movement into the illuminative way is gaged by the change in a Chrisitan's prayer more than anything else. As I stated earlier, the change from meditation to meditative-contemplation is the evidence and the catalyst of the change. This creates changes in the whole person and throughout the human dimensions. These changes are often misunderstood and resisted due to the natural tendency of homeostasis in the human being. As Dr. Frankl has stated, homeostasis is not the way of preferred health for the human being. The dynamic tension between a work to be done and the change it evokes is that which promotes a healthy human being. Being aware of one's "purpose in life" is the result of this dynamic tension and is more often than not, destroyed by homeostasis. It is in the balance of these tensions and not in the elimination of tension, that health is found.

The changes that are key to this transition are changes in the primary methods of meaning discovery in the various human dimensions. The awareness of God as truly alive and genuinely present changes the relationship that we have with God throughout the whole human being.

	Purgative Way	Illuminative Way	Unitive Way
Somatic Dimension	Attitudinal Values	Creative Values	
Psychic Dimension	Experiential Values	Attitudinal Values	
Noetic Dimension	Creative Values	Experiential Values	

Figure 12

In the illuminative way, the primary method of meaning discovery in the somatic dimension is related to creative values. The body, having suffered through the changes of becoming a true Christian, i.e. shedding old habits and relationships and establishing new habits and relationships, is now occupied with creating a new way of life in relationship to God. It is at work discovering new and more meaningful ways to express the genuineness of God's reality and presence in the Christian's life. It is learning to express the value of praise and worship. It is learning to serve others. It is learning what it means to be present in times of trial, challenge and joy. It is learning how to express the fruit of the Spirit as the genuine presence of God. It is learning the high value of physical presence in the process of spiritual growth, both the presence of God with the Christian and the presence of the Christian in relationship and ministry.

During the illuminative way, the psychic dimension finds its primary relationship to meaning discovery through attitudinal values. A Christian often enters this dimension through an experience that accompanies or ushers in the change and quite often, the Christian may misunderstand the place of the experience seeing it as the cause of the transition and change rather than the result of the transition and change. When that occurs, the Christian often becomes an advocate of a particular experience rather than a person who can grow through this change. This type of misunderstanding has been the cause of much contention and frustration in Christian history.

Examples would include the Wesleyan movement that focused on sanctification and holiness as the experience of this transition and the pentecostal movement that focused on the exercise of a particular gift of the Spirit as sign of the transition. Both of these movements gave rise to a number of Christian denominations built a least in part around a particular understanding of the focus of the movement. This transition causes some degree of suffering to be the focus of the psychic dimension as mind must learn to "mellow out" and identify the difference between the presence of God and the "experience" of the presence of God.

It is often said that Christians should be "locked up for six months" following this transition to keep them from doing undue damage to those around them. This transition is so strong in the psychic dimension, particularly the affective part of the psychic dimension, that the help of another, more mature Christian person can be a great help during this time. A spiritual guide or friend who understands the nature of the feelings and the realization of the genuineness of God's presence in this transition to the illuminative way, can truly help a Christian new to this transition to make a more mature movement forward through this time. It is a period of true suffering for the mind as it is prone to put itself forward, yet needs to see itself in a more proper relationship to the other human dimensions.

There is a great temptation to remain in this place, spiritually, and to seek to "enlighten" others as to how they, too, can experience the same sense of joy and zeal that the Christian, new to this transition, has found for him or herself. Benedict Groeschel quotes Thomas Merton from a posthumously published essay entitled *Contemplation in a World of Action:*

> The real point of the contemplative life has always been a deepening of faith and of the personal dimensions of liberty and apprehension to the point where our direct union with God is realized and "experienced." We awaken not only to a realization of the immensity and majesty of God "out there" as King and Ruler of the universe (which He is) but also a more intimate and more wonderful perception of Him as directly and personally present in our own being. Yet this is not a pantheistic merger or confusion of our being with His. On the contrary, there is a distinct conflict in the realization that though in some sense He is more truly ourselves than we are, yet we are not identical with Him, and though He loves us better than we can love ourselves we are opposed to Him, and in opposing Him we oppose our own deepest selves. If we are involved only in our surface existence, in externals, and in the trivial concerns of our ego, we are untrue to Him and to ourselves. To reach a true awareness of Him as well as ourselves, we have to renounce our selfish and limited self and enter into a whole new kind of existence, discovering an inner center of motivation and love which makes us see ourselves and everything else in an entirely new light (Groeschel, 1984, p. 137).

This is the struggle of the mind to see itself in relationship to that "new center" that is establishing the reality of His presence in us. This suffering is the same as the meaning of the suffering and death of Christ upon the cross for the Christian. It is an experience of suffering that helps to create a new center in the Christian's life. In Franklian terms, it is the attitude that we take toward this unavoidable suffering that determines whether or not we will find the meaning that is present there.

In the illuminative way the primary method of meaning discovery in the noetic dimension is in the area of experiencial values. The human spirit is experiencing the relationship of love with God. The Christian understands that "God is love" (I John 4:16, NIV). The Christian also understands that God is spirit and those who worship God must do so in spirit and in truth (John 4:24, NIV). It is in the dimension of the human spirit, the noetic dimension, that the human being makes genuine contact with the presence of God. It is the *Spirit* himself that testifies (bears witness) with our *spirit* that we are children of God (Romans 8:16, NIV). It is in the noetic dimension in the illuminative way that this love becomes a life-changing reality.

The power of this love is what establishes God as the center of the Christian's life. It is at this point that the Christian finds that the presence of God is more of a motivation for life than one's own anxieties and fears. The power of this experience is the power of love. It is harnessed in the noetic dimension and developed through a dynamic relationship of love with God. This provides more fuel to the temptation to remain at this level of spiritual maturity. It "feels" good and it "feels" right to have this relationship with God be the center of one's own living. The problem with remaining here is that one has to learn to disregard one's own "inner turmoil" in order to remain fixed on the wonderful parts of this stage of spiritual maturation.

While it becomes easier in many respects to pray and to do good works during this time in the spiritual life, it is also a time where our own inconsistencies become more and more apparent to us. The same love that draws us forward and away from our self-centeredness and anxieties, shines its penetrating light on the remainder of our lives in such a way that our inconsistencies become "illuminated" for us. When allowed to do its work, this love draws us forward toward the necessary dark night(s) of the soul and the dark night of the spirit that will come following the next transition into the unitive way. Let us turn now to the methods of meaning discovery that are exhibited as primary during the unitive way.

Methods of Meaning Discovery in the Unitive Way

	Purgative Way	Illuminative Way	Unitive Way
Somatic Dimension	Attitudinal Values	Creative Values	Experiential Values
Psychic Dimension	Experiential Values	Attitudinal Values	Creative Values
Noetic Dimension	Creative Values	Experiential Values	Attitudinal Values

Figure 13

Figure 13 displays the final shifting of the primary methods of meaning discovery that are experienced in the human dimensions during the transition to the unitive way. The primary focus of the somatic dimension during the unitive way is found in experiential values. The Christian in union with God will demonstrate through his or her very "being" the presence and meaning of God. In this way, he or she will be "like Christ." Since Jesus is "what God means" (the logos), the Christian who is in union with God will be an example of "what God means" as well.

Since it is the somatic dimension through which the human being relates and communicates with the real (physical) world in which he or she lives, it is in this dimension that the love of God will be demonstrated to the world. For the Christian, the body will be present and at work demonstrating the way in which God cares about all that God has created. Through what is said and what is done, the somatic dimension will find its primary meaning in demonstrating God's love to the world.

Those in union with God seem to be able to place themselves in places where they can care for the people and things that God has created. They live out their "high calling" to make the world a better place in which to live by completing those acts of charity that are before them. For the Christian in union with God, acts of charity make up the entirety of the Christian's life. It is, indeed, a ministry that is lived out in the somatic dimension.

The primary method of meaning discovery for the psychic dimension during the unitive way is found in creative values. The human mind seems to be designed for this very function. Through its processes of volition, rationalization, and conceptualization, the psychic dimension is able to take its understandings of meanings past, present, and (anticipated) future and create new thoughts and new vistas of meaning for the human being to act upon. In the unitive way, the psychic dimension is dreaming up new ways to make the presence of God known in the moment, giving rise to a way to appreciate the meaning of the moment in the truest sense of the word. To appreciate something or someone is to make them more valuable. When we participate in creating new ways to identify and participate in the meaning of the moment, we are truly appreciating it.

New ways of redeeming creation are dreamed and begun by persons who participate in the meaning of the moment. This creative activity is present in persons of all levels of spiritual maturity for creative values are natural to the human mind. However, while this activity is available to all who understand their psychological assets, it is not used by most for redemptive reasons. It is when a person moves through the unitive way into union with God that this type of meaning discovery is most at home in the human mind which is so richly prepared for it.

The primary method of meaning discovery for the noetic dimension during the unitive way is found in attitudinal values. In particular, the value of the attitude we take toward suffering defines this level of spiritual maturity for the noetic dimension. This is the time where "suffering with Christ" is most fully understood by the Christian. For it is during this time that the Christian is actually participating in the sufferings of Christ.

The noetic dimension is the one dimension that is equipped to deal with suffering. There are more resources for dealing with suffering in the noetic dimension than in either of the other two human dimensions. Meaning that goes beyond our limited understanding is essential for those who are to live in this world surrounded by its injustices and its inequities. If one were to try to deal with these challenges by trying to make sense of them, sanity would need to be sacrificed in the end. Only the noetic dimension gives Christians the framework from which to absorb and be absorbed into meaning that goes beyond understanding. This is the type of meaning that gives rise to forgiveness and sacrifice, two elements essential to the healing of people and their relationship to the world around them.

As we see in Figure 13, the unitive way is the place where the methods of meaning discovery are at home in the dimensions where they are able to most fully relate a person to meaning itself. It is the process of change in the movement of these primary methods of meaning discovery during the Christian's spiritual formation that can be resisted, thereby resisting the change necessary to become a whole and healthy spiritual person. Many times a person will want to hang on to that with which a person is familiar. This resistance to change will delay or even halt a person's spiritual growth, keeping him or her from becoming what they were created to be.

When recognized and embraced, these changes can help a Christian move through the transitions necessary in the movement forward in Christian spiritual formation to maturity. It should be helpful to know that one will naturally experience a change in the primary method of meaning discovery in different dimensions of the human life when a Christian is drawn on toward spiritual maturity.

CHAPTER VIII
ARE CHRISTIANS REALLY HELPED BY THIS INFORMATION?

The hypothesis that Christians would benefit from a meaning matrix formed by the application of Franklian psychology to the Christian spiritual formation methodology known as the three ways is validated by the study and research that preceded the writing of this book. The research verified that a majority of those Christians who participated in the study indicated by their answers on the pre-workshop questionnaire and the post-workshop questionnaire that such was the case for them.

The research data consists of answers gathered from a group of 40 participants. The total group was comprised of people who attended one of three different seminar workshops on Christian spiritual formation. The workshops were given over a period of six months in the fall of 2007 and the spring of 2008. The workshops included the basic information that is included in this book; i.e., a short history of Franklian psychology, Franklian dimensional ontology, the methods of meaning discovery, an overview of the three ways, and the establishment of a meaning matrix.

Gathering of the Data

The instruments used to gather the information were created from the information gathered from a Spiritual Formation Workshop Evaluation Questionnaire (see Appendix B). This questionnaire was distributed to 20 people: five logotherapists, five theological educators, five psychologists, and five pastors. The return rate was 100%. The answers given were numerical and were averaged. Those questions which received an overall rating of important, very important, or essential, were included in the pre-workshop questionnaire and post-workshop questionnaire.

Participants were asked to complete a Pre-Workshop Questionnaire at the beginning of the workshop and a Post-Workshop Questionnaire at the conclusion of the workshop (see Appendix C). Participation was about 90%. Those who completed both questionnaires were included in this study.

The age, gender, and denominational background of the participants was as follows:
Male = 33%,
Female = 67%,
Those over 60 years of age = 75%
Those 48-60 years of age = 17%
Those 31-45 years of age = 8%
Those under 31 years of age = 0%
United Methodist = 100%
Other denominations = 0%

Of those listing their current denominational affiliation as United Methodist, 60% listed from two to six other denominations in which they had also held membership. Six of ten of the United Methodists in this study had come into the United Methodist Church from another denomination. The other denominations included Church of Christ, Disciples of Christ, Baptist, Lutheran, Roman Catholic, Presbyterian, and non-denominational. Some participants had held membership in as many as four other denominations at some point in their lives.

The Pre-Workshop Questionnaire consisted of some biographical information, nine self-analysis questions where participants were asked to rate themselves in relationship to others concerning their knowledge of certain areas, and 17 information questions which helped to verify the amount of knowledge that the participant had in various areas.

The Post-Workshop Questionnaire consisted of the same (or extremely similar) questions with the inclusion of two additional self-analysis questions that pertained to the workshop, itself. That made a total of 11 self-analysis questions and 17 information questions on this questionnaire. The answers to both questionnaires were compared and examined.

Analysis of the Data

One significant observation from the data is the number of people who increased their ability to identify and understand the transitions in the Christian spiritual life. 48% of the participants were able to correctly identify the significant transitions in the Christian spiritual life following the workshop. Only eight percent had the correct answers both before and after the workshop. Nine out of ten of the remaining 50% of the participants were able to identify two of the three transitions even though they were unable to identify all three transitions. This shows a marked increase in the number of participants who obtained a knowledge of the significant transitions in the Christian spiritual life at the workshop.

A second observation was the number of people who moved down in their estimation of their knowledge of the Christian spiritual life. Over one-third of the participants lowered their estimation of their knowledge of Christian spiritual formation following the workshop. This is an indication that they had overestimated their knowledge of Christian spiritual formation in the beginning. Their comments following the workshop supported the fact that they had little if any idea in the beginning of the history or the depth of Christian spiritual formation. **They simply believed that their long tenure as a Christian somehow qualified them to know about Christian spiritual formation.** The knowledge that they gained in the workshop was enough to help them realize that they did not know as much about Christian spiritual formation as they first thought they did.

It was my initial expectation that a large number of the participants would have a small amount of knowledge at the most of Franklian psychology or Franklian philosophy. This expectation was confirmed with the data. In the information questions concerning Franklian dimensional ontology and its relationship to the three ways, the increase was between 30% and 58%. This large increase was verified by the final two self-analysis questions on the Post-Workshop Questionnaire. The final two questions dealt with how the workshop aided in understanding the purpose of and transitions in the Christian spiritual life and how much the information gained would affect the future development of the participant's own Christian spiritual life. 70% of the participants indicated that this information would affect the future development of their Christian spiritual lives "quite a bit" or "significantly."

CHAPTER IX
APPLICATION AND USES
OF THE MEANING MATRIX

The application and uses of the meaning matrix are applied most directly to those interested in Christian spiritual formation or those pursuing Christian spiritual maturity. The larger view of the application of Franklian psychology to the three ways is something that will help spiritual directors or spiritual friends as they work with Christians who are moving toward spiritual maturity within the context of a community of faith. There are restrictions to the use of this information when trying to apply it to oneself.

Challenge of Personal Analysis
Inability of Personal Assessment

The nature of personal relationship is such that no one can have a true opinion of his or her own actions that is other than a subjective opinion. Since we participate in our own thought processes before we choose to act or communicate with others, our relationship with others is always understood differently by others than it is by us. Others do not get to participate in or share our understanding of our thought processes. We may choose to think that we understand our relationship better because we understand what we "meant" and not just what we said or did, but the relationship is best judged by those who are the recipients of our words and actions.

We can only give an understanding of what we intended and are not in the position to determine an objective understanding of any relationship we have. This includes not only our relationships with others, or with the things around us, but also our relationship with God. For that reason, it is not advisable for anyone to try to assess his or her own spiritual maturity. The true assessment of one's own spiritual maturity is best done by the community of faith and by those who are trained spiritual directors or spiritual friends. The person who seeks to assess his or her own spiritual maturity will find their assessment skewed by their understanding of their intentions.

Need for Community Assessment

There is a need for assessment of one's spiritual maturity if a Christian is ever to move ahead with intentionality toward spiritual maturity. I believe that there is both a psychological reason and a spiritual reason for a human being to be drawn forward toward his or her own wholeness. Since the assessment of one's spiritual maturity is unable to be done with objectivity by the person involved in the process of maturity, it makes sense that there is a need for a process of community assessment in order to help and encourage Christians in their movement forward in spiritual maturity.

A variety of methods are possible. Small groups that function as accountability groups can help a person receive valuable feedback concerning how well his or her intentions are being turned into realities. Community encouragement within the context of corporate ministry endeavors can help one recognize his or her progress. When we work together for the accomplishment of a common good, words of encouragement and words of affirmation can help further our understanding of how our spiritual maturity is being perceived.

Our relationships with those in need will help us to recognize our spiritual maturity. The needs of others and our ability to discern those needs and become involved with them will serve as a valuable instructor concerning our spiritual maturity. It makes little difference whether the needs of others are physical, mental, or spiritual in nature, our relationship with those in need will show us our own maturity. The value of this involvement is enhanced if we are able to share our learning and our understanding with others who have experienced the same type of growth or those who currently are involved in the same type of experiences. Both may be necessary to keep us from a situation of the "blind leading the blind."

Use for Pastoral Assessment

Pastors are among those most in need of the ability to accurately and helpfully assess where Christians are in the process of spiritual formation to maturity. It is inherent in the job of the pastor to be able to help Christians grow forward spiritually.

Use in Assessing Others

The application of Franklian psychology to the three ways should be a great help to pastors in their work with Christians who are involved in spiritual maturation. A knowledge of Franklian dimensional ontology, the methods of meaning discovery, and a general understanding of the three ways, including the psychological overlay of Benedict Groeschel will all help a pastor to be better able to understand the challenges and changes that face those for whom he or she cares.

This knowledge will be helpful when a pastor encounters a Christian who seems to be stuck in one area or another, unable to understand or move through the changes that face him or her. Kind explanation and encouragement concerning the types of prayer that might be explored may help move such a person forward. When a pastor encounters a Christian who is anxious about the changes they face or is upset about some darkness that he or she faces, it should be a great help to share how this is all a part of a greater plan for growth, and be able to share other instances where such change and even darkness have been the tools of God's preparation in the process of spiritual maturity.

This information should also be valuable as a teaching aid for pastors who seek to further the interest of Christians in the process of spiritual maturity. Many Christians may feel a need to become more than they are in respect to their ideas of what a

Christian is or is supposed to be and yet have little if any idea of how to move forward. Pastors should be able to teach and encourage Christians to grow forward in spiritual maturity that they might become the people that they were created to be.

Need for Education and Assessment Tools

There is a genuine need for assessment tools to help pastors, spiritual guides and spiritual friends who understand the value of this type of meaning matrix. It is beyond the scope of this book to prepare, test, and produce such assessment tools, but they are greatly needed. Tools for education will also help with assessment. Many Christians are simply unaware of the existence of the three ways and of Franklian psychology. In the seminars that I have taught, people get excited to realize that other Christians have made this journey in quest of spiritual maturity before and have left a path with signposts all along the way. They are excited to realize that there is a credible source in the field of psychology for the tri-partite nature of the human being and they cherish the understanding of dimensional ontology and the methods of meaning discovery. Many times even before the seminar is over, they are busy using this "new-found" knowledge to assess their own situations and even though this is a dangerous thing in many respects, indicating the pervasiveness of the culture of "selfism," it also shows the ability of people to comprehend and apply this knowledge in the area of spiritual formation. There is a genuine hunger for spiritual formation with depth and substance. It is my hope that this meaning matrix can help meet some of that hunger and provide another view into spiritual formation that contains the kind of depth and substance that will last through the changes of time and cultures to continue to point people toward the wholeness of Christ.

Use for Community of Faith Assessment

This meaning matrix can be used by communities of faith in valuable ways. It can serve as the foundation of training for pastors, spiritual guides and spiritual friends. It can help in the training of Christian counselors who need to be able to discern times of spiritual darkness and change that are normal to the process of spiritual growth.

Training for Pastors, Spiritual Guides, and Spiritual Friends

The application of Franklian psychology to the three ways and the resultant meaning matrix can be used to help train pastors for their work with Christians who are desirous of spiritual growth as well as those Christians in whom a pastor may discern a latent interest in or need for spiritual growth. No one has access to the human soul of another as readily as a pastor. Training for pastors which would include the information necessary for understanding the meaning matrix as well as the use of the meaning matrix itself could be very helpful in their work with Christians interested in spiritual formation.

Spiritual guides are most frequently pastors with specialized training in spiritual formation. Many have various levels of training in counseling as well. Their work with Christians is more directed and less general than the work of a pastor. A spiritual guide is one who is sought out for the benefit of another. Usually an agreement is entered into with a spiritual guide for the benefit of another. The agreement will differ according to the relationship but it will at least include time together for communication around the desire to grow toward spiritual maturity. In some cases, spiritual guides are assigned to persons such as pastors in order to make certain that spiritual growth is intentional in the life agenda of that person.

Spiritual guides could use general training on the information necessary to understand and use the meaning matrix. In addition, spiritual guides could benefit from some intentional oversight as they meet with those whom they are helping.

Spiritual friends are very similar to spiritual guides with the exception that they are usually not pastors and usually not ordained. Spiritual friends are persons who are sought out with the intent to make spiritual formation an intentional part of a friendship relationship. Spiritual friends are usually older, wiser, and more mature than those who seek their spiritual friendship for the purpose of intentional spiritual growth.

Spiritual friends could benefit from the same training concerning the knowledge necessary for the understanding of the meaning matrix and for an understanding of the use of the meaning matrix to help assess the movement toward spiritual maturity of their friends. While they could also benefit from collegial relationships with other trained spiritual friends, they would most likely have less time for and less need of an organized relationship of intentional oversight.

Training for Spiritual Counselors

Training which included an understanding of the information presented in this dissertation would be helpful for spiritual counselors. Spiritual counselors have a professional relationship with their clients for the purpose of benefiting the client. It would be a great advantage for a spiritual counselor to have a truly workable knowledge of the information necessary to understand the meaning matrix as well as the ability to use the meaning matrix to help assess the needs of their clients.

Spiritual counselors are trained to bring many resources to bear upon the challenges and needs of their clients. The use of Franklian psychology, the three ways, and the resultant meaning matrix would be a helpful addition to the resources of spiritual counselors. This information would be helpful to both Christian and non-Christian counselors who deal with Christian clients. A working knowledge of the significant transitions in the Christian spiritual life would be beneficial to anyone who works with Christian clientele.

CHAPTER X
CONCLUSION

Christians from the first century forward have intentionally sought spiritual formation in the image of Christ. The search has been referred to as a "journey" by some and a "quest" by others. Those who highlight the process and practice of spiritual formation gravitate toward defining it as a journey. Those who see the possibility of being formed in the image of Christ in this lifetime gravitate toward defining it as a quest. Both groups would benefit from a better understanding of the times of transition in the Christian spiritual life. This understanding is exactly what is offered through the establishment of a meaning matrix for Christian spiritual growth through the use of Franklian psychology.

The use of Franklian psychology in the establishment of a meaning matrix for Christian spiritual formation is a definite help to anyone seeking to more thoroughly understand the significant transitions in Christian spiritual formation as presented in the three ways. Franklian psychology helps specifically with a more developed understanding of human dimensional ontology and the methods of meaning discovery. The meaning matrix helps one understand the movement through the significant transitions in the Christian spiritual life by helping one understand the primary methods of meaning discovery found in the various dimensions of the human being during those times of significant transition. My experience with Christian spiritual formation workshops and the data that I have gathered convinces me that an understanding of the factors addressed in this study will positively affect the future of one's Christian spiritual life.

I have also concluded that this information would be beneficial to all of those helping professions that deal with the development of the spiritual nature of the human being. The clergy, educators, and those working in the healing professions who deal with a Christian clientele would greatly benefit from having a working knowledge of the elements that go into the making of the meaning matrix as well as the meaning matrix, itself. It is hoped that the power of meaning to affect positive change in the lives of human beings has been affirmed in this study.

Areas for Further Development

Areas for further study should include the validation, application, and use of the meaning matrix. In order to further validate the meaning matrix, studies should be done with Christians who have moved through the three ways to further verify the primary methods of meaning discovery within the various human dimensions before and following movement through those significant transitions. Even though this process would be somewhat subjective (as is much of what goes on in the analysis of spiritual life), the study is possible and would help to further strengthen the conclusions.

Application of the meaning matrix to those persons who are experiencing the significant transitions of the Christian spiritual life would be the ground of more fruitful study. Further study could help determine how much it would benefit Christians to know about these transitions before and during the times that they are experiencing them.

Use of the meaning matrix to help Christians further understand the nature of Christian spiritual growth and to help those who work with Christians who are moving forward in their spiritual growth would be beneficial, also. What seems to be lacking most in the lives of those with whom I have worked is a general overall understanding of the purpose and path of Christian spiritual formation. Those who have worked with the meaning matrix have found that the information necessary to understanding the meaning matrix and the meaning matrix, itself, both provide an overall understanding of Christian spiritual formation that is deeply meaningful and truly helpful. In the end, that is the true value of this study.

Appendix A

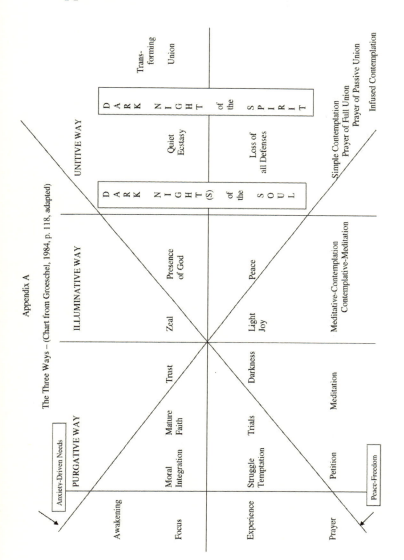

Appendix A

The Three Ways – (Chart from Groeschel, 1984, p. 118, adapted)

Appendix B

Appendix B is a copy of the Workshop Evaluation Questionnaire. It was sent to 20 people who are knowledgeable in the fields of Franklian psychology and/or the Christian religion. The purpose of the questionnaire was to help determine those questions that would be important, very important or essential to include in the Pre-Workshop Questionnaire and Post-Workshop Questionnaire. The numbers listed here represent the average score of the responses given to each question.

<u>Spiritual Formation Workshop Evaluation Questionnaire</u>

Please indicate your answer to the following question as it relates to the statements below and return to me at this e-mail address. (wwds@sbcglobal.net) Your help is essential in establishing a meaningful and valid questionnaire for both the pre-test and post-test work on this subject. Thank you for your participation.

Question:

In evaluating the factors that aid a person's understanding of <u>the purpose of</u> and <u>transitions in</u> the Christian spiritual life that can be positively affected by the application of Franklian psychology, how important do you believe it is to know a person's opinion concerning the following information? Please evaluate using the following scale:
    5 = essential
    4 = very important
    3 = important
    2 = not important
    1 = not necessary at all

CONCERNING THE CHRISTIAN SPIRITUAL LIFE:

___ A person's rating of their own understanding of Christian spiritual formation.
___ The purpose of Christian spiritual formation.
___ The history of Christian spiritual formation.
___ The importance of understanding "the three ways."
___ The psychology of Christian spiritual formation.
___ The spiritual disciplines that aid Christian spiritual formation.
___ A person's own involvement with the spiritual disciplines.

CONCERNING FRANKLIAN PSYCHOLOGY:

___ A person's rating of their own understanding of Franklian psychology.
___ A brief history of Viktor Frankl.
___ The development of Logotherapy.
___ The principles of Logotherapy.
___ Franklian dimensional ontology.
___ Franklian methods of meaning discovery.

CONCERNING THE ONTOLOGICAL MAKEUP OF THE HUMAN BEING:

___ A person's rating of their own understanding of human ontology.
___ Franklian dimensional ontology.
___ A history of Christian spiritual ontology.

Franklian Psychology

- ___ The interaction between the specifically human dimensions.
- ___ Various schools of thought concerning the human dimensions.
- ___ How psychology relates to human ontology.

CONCERNING THE NATURE OF MEANING AND ITS RELATIONSHIP TO GOD:

- ___ A person's rating of their own understanding of the nature of meaning.
- ___ Frankl's understanding of the nature of meaning.
- ___ The methods of meaning discovery.
- ___ The relationship of meaning discovery to the stages of spiritual formation.

CONCERNING THE SPECIFIC TRANSITIONS IN THE CHRISTIAN SPIRITUAL LIFE:

- ___ A person's rating of their own understanding of the transitions.
- ___ Movement through the purgative way.
- ___ Movement through the illuminative way.
- ___ Movement through the unitive way.
- ___ The relationship of prayer to these transitions.
- ___ The relationship of meditation to these transitions.
- ___ The relationship of contemplation to these transitions.
- ___ The relationship of the prayer of passive union to these transitions.
- ___ The relationship of creativity to these transitions.
- ___ The relationship of suffering to these transitions.

___ The relationship of experiential love to these transitions.

THANK YOU FOR YOUR PARTICIPATION!

Appendix C

The samples of the Pre-Workshop and Post-Workshop Questionnaires are listed in Appendix C.

Pre-Workshop Questionnaire

Instructions: Please complete the questionnaire as completely as possible. Answer each question to the best of your understanding. Return the completed questionnaire in the enclosed, stamped, and addressed envelope. (If you have misplaced the envelope, please return to: **Dr. Randy L. Scraper, 3344 Cheyenne Drive, Woodward, Oklahoma, 73801.**) Data gathered through the use of this questionnaire will be analyzed and used in a PhD dissertation. All personal information will be kept confidential.

Biographical Information:

Name: _____

Gender: Male   Female

Age: 18 or below   19 – 30   31-45   46 – 60   Beyond 60

Number of years you have been a Christian:

5 or less   6 – 12   13 – 25   26 – 40   Beyond 40

Denominational Affiliation(s): Mark those denominations in which you have been an active participant.

_____ United Methodist _____ Presbyterian
_____ Disciples of Christ _____ Church of Christ
_____ Pentecostal _____ Roman Catholic

_____ Baptist _____ Eastern Orthodox
_____ Other Catholic
_____ Other Protestant _____ Non-Denominational

Questions:

1. How would you rank your knowledge of Christian Spiritual formation?
   ___ Much Below Average
   ___ Below Average
   ___ Average
   ___ Above Average
   ___ Much Above Average

2. How would you rank your knowledge of "The Three Ways?"
   ___ Much Below Average
   ___ Below Average
   ___ Average
   ___ Above Average
   ___ Much Above Average

3. Which **three** of the following would be included in a fundamental understanding of "The Three Ways?"

___ Justification ___ Trepidation
___ Illumination ___ Forgiveness
___ Purgation ___ Sanctification
___ Glorification ___ Union
___ Justice ___ Mercy
___ Grace ___ Ascension

4. Which of these best describes your understanding of the purpose of Christian spiritual formation?

___ To be formed in the image of Christ
___ To become one with God
___ To be a better Christian
___ To be a better servant of Christ in this world
___ To glorify the risen Savior
___ To be in union with God

5. Do you practice spiritual disciplines religiously? (More than occasionally.)
___ Yes ___ No

6. Which spiritual disciplines do you practice religiously?

___ Private prayer ___ Reading the Bible
___ Devotional reading ___ Bible study
___ Journal writing ___ Acts of charity
___ Tithing ___ Giving
___ Group prayer ___ Public worship

___ Service to others   ___ Church life
___ Meditation   ___ Contemplation
___ Discernment

7. Which five of these spiritual disciplines do you consider most important? Number them 1 through 5 in order of their importance with 1 being the most important, 2 the next most important, etc.

___ Private prayer   ___ Reading the Bible
___ Devotional reading   ___ Bible study
___ Journal writing   ___ Acts of charity
___ Tithing   ___ Giving
___ Group prayer   ___ Public worship
___ Service to others   ___ Church life
___ Meditation   ___ Contemplation
___ Discernment

8. Which of these statements best describes your understanding of the relationship between the experience of love in the presence of God and the anxiety and fear related to human nature?

___ Love overcomes fear at the beginning of the Christian life.
___ Love overcomes fear early in the Christian life.
___ Love overcomes fear late in the Christian life.
___ Love never really overcomes fear in the Christian life.
___ Love overcomes fear at a critical transition in the Christian life.

Franklian Psychology

9. How would you rank your knowledge of Franklian psychology?

   ____ Much Below Average
   ____ Below Average
   ____ Average
   ____ Above Average
   ____ Much Above Average

10. Which of the following are true about Dr. Viktor Frankl? Viktor Frankl was:

    ____ A Viennese psychiatrist.
    ____ A student of Adler.
    ____ A student of Freud.
    ____ A doctor of philosophy.
    ____ A brain surgeon.
    ____ A survivor of four concentration camps.
    ____ A survivor of two concentration camps.
    ____ All of the above.
    ____ None of the above.

11. Which of these phrases best describes Logotherapy?

    ____ An alternative to psychotherapy.
    ____ Feeling oriented therapy.
    ____ Meaning centered therapy.
    ____ A form of existential therapy.
    ____ Therapy based on a book written by Dr. Frankl.

12. Which of the following are considered principles of Logotherapy?

___ Freedom of thought ___ Freedom of the will
___ Freedom of action ___ Will to action
___ Will to meaning ___ Will to thinking
___ Meaning of life ___ Meaning of purpose
___ Meaning of the will

13. How would you rank your knowledge of human dimensional ontology?

    ___ Much Below Average
    ___ Below Average
    ___ Average
    ___ Above Average
    ___ Much Above Average

14. Which of these best describes your understanding of the dimensions of the human being?

    ___ Body and Soul   ___ Body and Spirit
    ___ Body, Soul, and Spirit   ___ Body and Mind
    ___ Body, Mind, and Spirit   ___ Body, Mind, & Soul
    ___ Soul and Spirit

15. Which is the largest of the human dimensions?

    ___ Somatic   ___ Psychic
    ___ Noetic

16. Where are the most resources found for meaning discovery?

Franklian Psychology

___ Somatic   ___ Psychic
___ Noetic

17. Which of these mental/emotional activities happens at the point of interaction between two of the human dimensions?

    ___ Volition   ___ Rationalization
    ___ Conceptualization   ___ Revelation

18. How would you rank your knowledge of the transitions in the Christian spiritual life?

    ___ Much Below Average
    ___ Below Average
    ___ Average
    ___ Above Average
    ___ Much Above Average

19. Are you aware of specific transitions in the Christian spiritual life?

    ___ Yes   ___ No

20. Which of the following would you name as transitions in the Christian Spiritual life?

    ___ Justification   ___ Sanctification
    ___ Glorification   ___ Illumination

___ Union   ___ Purgation
___ Petition   ___ Meditation
___ Contemplation

21. How would you rate your knowledge of meaning discovery?

    ___ Much Below Average
    ___ Below Average
    ___ Average
    ___ Above Average
    ___ Much Above Average

22. What are the areas of meaning discovery that are significant in Franklian psychology?

    ___ Creative   ___ Experiential
    ___ Unavoidable suffering ___ Imagination
    ___ Conceptualization
    ___ Pain and suffering

23. What do you believe is the single most motivational activity for Christian spiritual growth?

    ___ Prayer   ___ Bible study
    ___ Acts of charity   ___ Acts of mercy
    ___ Giving   ___ Tithing
    ___ Church participation ___ Public worship

24. How would you rank your knowledge of the purpose of Christian spiritual formation?

Franklian Psychology

___ Much Below Average
___ Below Average
___ Average
___ Above Average
___ Much Above Average

25. How would you rank your knowledge of the significant transitions in the Christian spiritual life?

    ___ Much Below Average
    ___ Below Average
    ___ Average
    ___ Above Average
    ___ Much Above Average

26. How has the use of Franklian psychology in the establishment of a meaning matrix aided your understanding of the purpose of and transitions in the Christian spiritual life?

    ___ Not at all
    ___ Very little
    ___ Somewhat
    ___ Quite a bit
    ___ Significantly

Appendix D

Post-Workshop Questionnaire

Instructions: Please complete the questionnaire as completely as possible. Answer each question to the best of your understanding. Return the completed questionnaire in the enclosed, stamped, and addressed envelope. (If you have misplaced the envelope,) please return to:

    Dr. Randy L. Scraper,
    3344 Cheyenne Drive,
    Woodward, Oklahoma, 73801.

Data gathered through the use of this questionnaire will be analyzed and used in a PhD dissertation. All personal information will be kept confidential.

Biographical Information:

Name:_____

Gender: Male   Female

Questions:

27.   How would you rank your knowledge of Christian Spiritual formation?

    ___ Much Below Average
    ___ Below Average
    ___ Average
    ___ Above Average
    ___ Much Above Average

28. How would you rank your knowledge of "The Three Ways?"

___ Much Below Average
___ Below Average
___ Average
___ Above Average
___ Much Above Average

29. Which **three** of the following would be included in a fundamental understanding of "The Three Ways?"

___ Justification   ___ Trepidation
___ Illumination   ___ Forgiveness
___ Purgation   ___ Sanctification
___ Glorification   ___ Union
___ Justice   ___ Mercy
___ Grace   ___ Ascension

30. Which of these best describes your understanding of the purpose of Christian Spiritual formation?

___ To be formed in the image of Christ
___ To become one with God
___ To be a better Christian
___ To be a better servant of Christ in this world
___ To glorify the risen Savior

___ To be in union with God

31. Do you practice spiritual disciplines religiously? (More than occasionally.)

___ Yes   ___ No

32. Which spiritual disciplines do you practice religiously?

___ Private prayer   ___ Reading Bible
___ Devotional reading   ___ Bible study
___ Journal writing   ___ Acts of charity
___ Tithing   ___ Giving
___ Group prayer   ___ Public worship
___ Service to others   ___ Church life
___ Meditation   ___ Contemplation
___ Discernment

33. Which five of these spiritual disciplines do you consider most important? Number them 1 through 5 in order of their importance with 1 being the most important, 2 the next most important, etc.

___ Private prayer   ___ Reading Bible
___ Devotional reading   ___ Bible study
___ Journal writing   ___ Acts of charity
___ Tithing   ___ Giving
___ Group prayer   ___ Public worship
___ Service to others   ___ Church life

Franklian Psychology

___ Meditation   ___ Contemplation
___ Discernment

34. Which of these statements best describes your understanding of the relationship between the experience of love in the presence of God and the anxiety and fear related to human nature?

     ___ Love overcomes fear at the beginning of the Christian life.
     ___ Love overcomes fear early in the Christian life.
     ___ Love overcomes fear late in the Christian life.
     ___ Love never really overcomes fear in the Christian life.
     ___ Love overcomes fear at a critical transition in the Christian life.

35. How would you rank your knowledge of Franklian psychology?

     ___ Much Below Average
     ___ Below Average
     ___ Average
     ___ Above Average
     ___ Much Above Average

36. Which of the following are true about Dr. Viktor Frankl? Viktor Frankl was:

     ___ A Viennese psychiatrist.
     ___ A student of Adler.
     ___ A student of Freud.
     ___ A doctor of philosophy.
     ___ A brain surgeon.

___ A survivor of four concentration camps.
___ A survivor of two concentration camps.
___ All of the above.
___ None of the above.

37. Which of these phrases best describes Logotherapy?

___ An alternative to psychotherapy.
___ Feeling oriented therapy.
___ Meaning centered therapy.
___ A form of existential therapy.
___ Therapy based on a book written by Dr. Frankl.

38. Which of the following are considered principles of Logotherapy?

___ Freedom of thought
___ Freedom of the will
___ Freedom of action
___ Will to action
___ Will to meaning
___ Will to thinking
___ Meaning of life
___ Meaning of purpose
___ Meaning of the will

39. How would you rank your knowledge of human dimensional ontology?

___ Much Below Average

___ Below Average
    ___ Average
    ___ Above Average
    ___ Much Above Average

40. Which of these best describes your understanding of the dimensions of the human being?

    ___ Body and Soul   ___ Body and Spirit
    ___ Body, Soul, and Spirit   ___ Body and Mind
    ___ Body, Mind, and Spirit
    ___ Body, Mind, and Soul   ___ Soul and Spirit

41. Which is the most inclusive of the human dimensions?

    ___ Somatic   ___ Psychic   ___ Noetic

42. Where are the most resources found for meaning discovery?

    ___ Somatic   ___ Psychic   ___ Noetic

43. Which of these mental/emotional activities happens at the point of interaction between two of the human dimensions?

    ___ Volition   ___ Rationalization
    ___ Conceptualization   ___ Revelation

44. How would you rank your knowledge of the transitions in the Christian spiritual life?

___ Much Below Average
___ Below Average
___ Average
___ Above Average
___ Much Above Average

45. Are you aware of specific transitions in the Christian spiritual life?

___ Yes   ___ No

46. Which of the following would you name as transitions in the Christian Spiritual life?

___ Justification   ___ Sanctification
___ Glorification   ___ Illumination
___ Union   ___ Purgation
___ Petition   ___ Meditation
___ Contemplation

47. How would you rate your knowledge of meaning discovery?

___ Much Below Average
___ Below Average
___ Average
___ Above Average

Franklian Psychology

___ Much Above Average

48. What are the areas of meaning discovery that are significant in Franklian psychology?

    ___ Creative   ___ Experiential
    ___ Unavoidable suffering   ___ Imagination
    ___ Conceptualization   ___ Pain and suffering

49. What do you believe is the single most motivational activity for Christian spiritual growth?

    ___ Prayer   ___ Bible study
    ___ Acts of charity   ___ Acts of mercy
    ___ Giving   ___ Tithing
    ___ Church participation   ___ Public worship

50. How would you rank your knowledge of the purpose of Christian spiritual formation?

    ___ Much Below Average
    ___ Below Average
    ___ Average
    ___ Above Average
    ___ Much Above Average

51. How would you rank your knowledge of the significant transitions in the Christian spiritual life?

___ Much Below Average
___ Below Average
___ Average
___ Above Average
___ Much Above Average

52. How has the use of Franklian psychology in the establishment of a meaning matrix aided your understanding of the purpose of and transitions in the Christian spiritual life?

___ Not at all
___ Very little
___ Somewhat
___ Quite a bit
___ Significantly

53. How has the workshop aided your understanding of the purpose of and transitions in the Christian spiritual life?

___ Much Below Average
___ Below Average
___ Average
___ Above Average
___ Much Above Average

54. How much would you say that the information gained in this workshop will affect the future development of your Christian spiritual life?

Franklian Psychology

___ Not at all
___ Very little
___ Somewhat
___ Quite a bit
___ Significantly

References

Beach, F. A. (2008). *The Descent of Instinct.* Psychol. Rev. 62:401-10. Retrieved June 10, 2008, at: Http://en.wikipedia.org/wiki/Instinct

Bible, (1978). New International Version, New York: International Bible Society.

Frankl, V. E. (1959). *Man's Search for Meaning.* New York: Washington Square Press.

Frankl, V. E. (1969). *The Will to Meaning: Foundations and Applications of Logotherapy.* New York: Meridian.

Frankl, V. E. (1975). *The Unconscious God.* New York: Simon and Schuster.

Frankl, V. E. (1978). *The Unheard Cry for Meaning: Psychotherapy and Humanism.* New York: Simon and Schuster.

Frankl, V. E. (1997). *Viktor Frankl recollections: An autobiography.* New York and London: Plenum Press.

Frankl, V. E. (1997). *Man's Search for Ultimate Meaning.* Cambridge: Persues Publishing.

Gay, P. (1988). *Freud: A Life for Our Times.* New York: Norton.

Gould, W. B. (1993). *Frankl: Life With Meaning.* Belmont: Brooks/Cole Publishing Company.

Graber, A. V. (2004). *Viktor Frankl's Logotherapy: Method of Choice in Ecumenical Pastoral Psychology.* Lima: Wyndham Hall Press.

Groeschel, B. J. (1984). *Spiritual Passages.* New York: Crossroad.

Kalmar, S. (1982). A brief history of Logotherapy. In Sandra A. Wawrytko (Ed), *Analecta Frankliana.* Berkeley, CA: Institute of Logotherapy Press.

Kielhofner, G. (2008). Volition. In Gary Kielhofner: *Model of Human Occupation: Theory and Application,* (4th ed.). Baltimore: Lippencott Williams and Wilkins. Retrieved June 4, 2008, at:Http://en.wikipedia.org/ wiki/Volition_%28psychology%29

Lukas, E. (1986). *Meaning in Suffering*. Berkeley, CA: Institute of Logotherapy Press.

Merton, T. (1973). *Contemplation in a World of Action*. New York: Doubleday Image.

Tanquerey, A. (1930). *The Spiritual Life: Ascetical Mystical Theology*. Tournai, Belgium: Desclee.

Underhill, E. (1911). *Mysticism*. New York: Image.

Van Kaam, A. (1989). *Fundamental Formation/Formative Spirituality*. New York: Crossroad.

Bibliography

Beach, F. A. (2008). *The Descent of Instinct.* Psychol. Rev. 62:401-10. Retrieved June 10, 2008, at: http://en.wikipedia.org/wiki/Instinct

Bible. (1978). New International Version. New York: International Bible Society.

Bowne, B. P. (1887). *Philosophy of Theism.* New York: Harper and Brothers.

Callen, B. L. (2001). *Authentic Spirituality: Moving beyond Mere Religion.* Grand Rapids: Baker Academic.

Crumbaugh, J. C. (1988). *Everything to Gain: A Guide to Self-Fulfillment through Logoanalysis.* Berkeley: Institute of Logotherapy Press.

Davis-Finck, M. M. and Gilmore-Finck, T. (Eds.). (1993). *Viktor Frankl and Logotherapy: Everything to Gain.* Saratoga: Institute of Logotherapy Press.

Dunn, J. D. G. (1970). *Baptism in the Holy Spirit.* Philadelphia: Westminster.

Fabry, J. B. (1968). *The Pursuit of Meaning.* Berkeley: Institute of Logotherapy Press.

Fabry, J. B.(1988). *Guideposts to Meaning.* Oakland: New Harbinger.

Frankl, V. E. (1959). *Man's Search for Meaning.* New York: Washington Square Press.

Frankl, V. E. (1967). *Psychotherapy and Existentialism.* New York: Washington Square Press.

Frankl, V. E. (1969). *The Will to Meaning: Foundations and Applications of Logotherapy.* New York: Meridian.

Frankl, V. E. (1975). *The Unconscious God.* New York: Simon and Schuster.

Frankl, V. E. (1978). *The Unheard Cry for Meaning: Psychotherapy and Humanism.* New York: Simon and Schuster.

Frankl, V. E. (1997). *Viktor Frankl recollections: An autobiography.* New York and London: Plenum Press.

Frankl, V. E. (1997). *Man's Search for Ultimate Meaning.* Cambridge: Persues Publishing.

Gay, P. (1988). *Freud: A Life for Our Times.* New York: Norton.

Gould, W. B. (1993). *Frankl: Life With Meaning.* Belmont: Brooks/Cole Publishing Company.

Graber, A. V. (2004). *Viktor Frankl's Logotherapy: Method of Choice in Ecumenical Pastoral Psychology.* Lima: Wyndham Hall Press.

Groeschel, B. J. (1984). *Spiritual Passages.* New York: Crossroad.

Jones, F. H. and Jones, J. K. (Eds.). *Victor Frankl's Logotherapy: Personal Conscience and Global Concern.* Berkeley: Institute of Logotherapy Press.

Kalmar, S. (1982). Introduction: A brief history of Logotherapy. In Sandra A. Wawrytko (Ed), *Analecta Frankliana.* (pp. XV-XXIV). Berkeley, CA: Institute of Logotherapy Press.

Klingaman, W. K. (1990). *The First Century.* New York: HarperCollins.

Kielhofner, G. Volition. In Gary Kielhofner: *Model of Human Occupation:Theory and application.* (4th ed.). Baltimore: Lippencott Williams and Wilkins. Retrieved June 4,2008,at:ttp://en.wikipedia.org/wiki/Volition%28 psychology%29

Lukas, E. (1986). *Meaning in Suffering.* Berkeley. CA: Institute of Logotherapy Press.

Lukas, E. (1984). *Meaningful Living.* New York: Grove Press.

McDonnell, K., and Montague, G. T. (1990). *Christian Initiation and Baptism in the Holy Spirit.* Collegeville, Minnesota: Liturgical Press.

Merton, T. (1973). *Contemplation in a World of Action.* New York: Doubleday Image.

Mott, M. (1984). *The Seven Mountains of Thomas Merton.* Boston: Houghton Mifflin.

St. John of the Cross. (1990). *Dark Night of the Soul.* (E. Allison Peers, trans.). New York: Image Press.

St. John of the Cross. (1987). *Selected Writings.* (K. Kavanaugh, O.C.D., Ed.). New York: Paulist Press.

Takashima, H. (1977). *Psychosomatic Medicine and Logotherapy.* Berkeley: Institute of Logotherapy Press.

Tanquerey, A. (1930). *The Spiritual Life: Ascetical Mystical Theology.* Tournai, Belgium: Desclee.

Underhill, E. (1911). *Mysticism.* New York: Image.

Van Kaam, A. (1989). *Fundamental Formation: Formative Spirituality.* New York: Crossroad.

Van Kaam, A. (1985). *Human Formation: Formative Spirituality.* New York: Crossroad.

Van Kaam, A. (1986). *Formation of the Human Heart: Formative Spirituality.* New York: Crossroad.

Van Kaam, A. (1984). *Spiritual Formation and Mysticism. Studies in Formative Spirituality,* Volume V (Number 1), 11-143.

Wawrytko, S. A. (1982). *Analecta Frankliana.* Berkeley: Institute of Logotherapy Press.

Yoder, J. D. (1989). *Meaning in Therapy: A Logotherapy Casebook for Counselors.* Columbus, GA: Institute of Logotherapy Press.

ABOUT THE AUTHOR

Dr. Randy L. Scraper is a United Methodist pastor with over thirty years of experience in churches that range in size from six members to over eight thousand members. He and his wife, Wanda, have three grown children and nine grandchildren. Dr. Scraper has a passion for preaching, teaching, and Christian spiritual formation. He holds the Diplomate credential with the Viktor Frankl Institute of Logotherapy and has served as adjunct faculty at Baker University and at Northwestern Oklahoma State University. He enjoys teaching seminars for pastors and laypersons. Dr. Scraper has maintained a lifelong interest in Kin no Ryu Kujutsu, a form of Karate in which he holds several black belts. His other interests include golf, chess, reading, writing, painting, gardening, model trains, and flying remote control airplanes.

Made in the USA
Middletown, DE
20 September 2021